AF380462

Rita Robillard
Time and Place

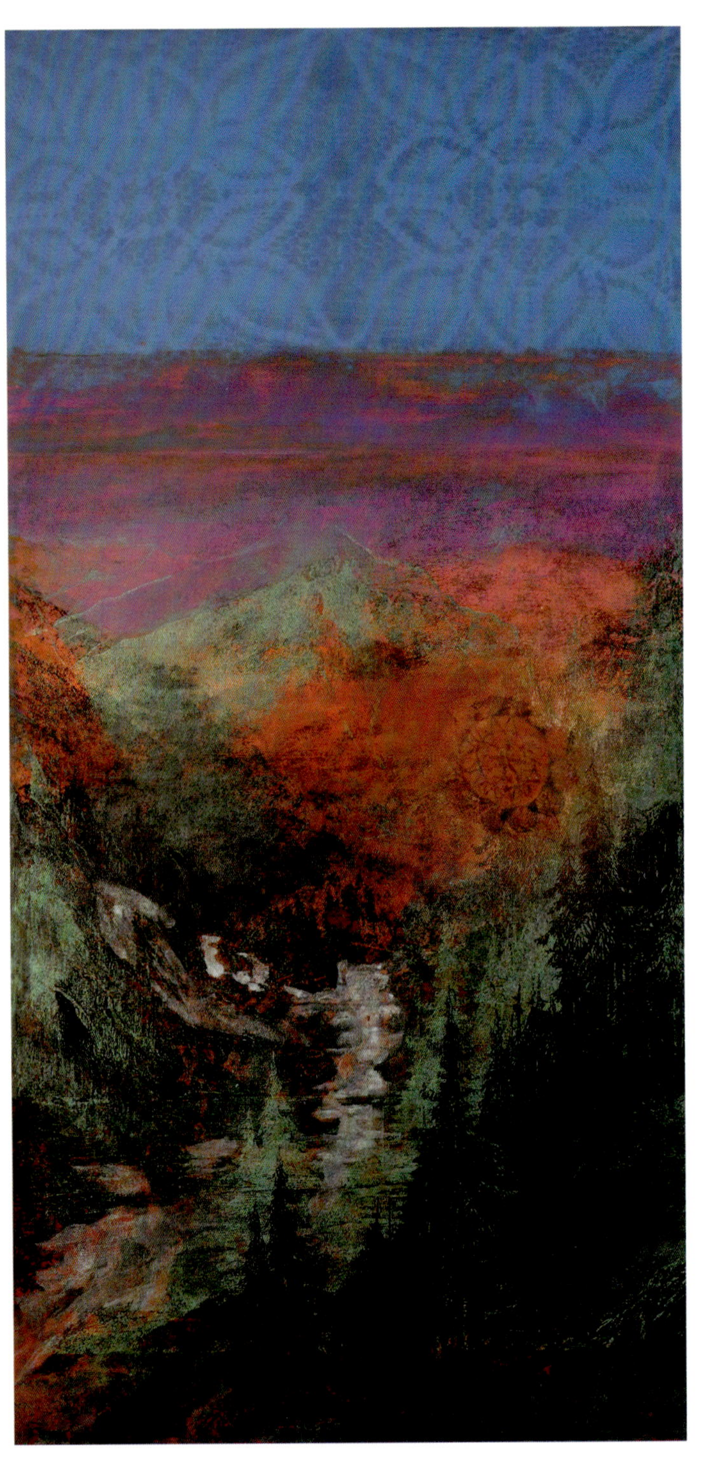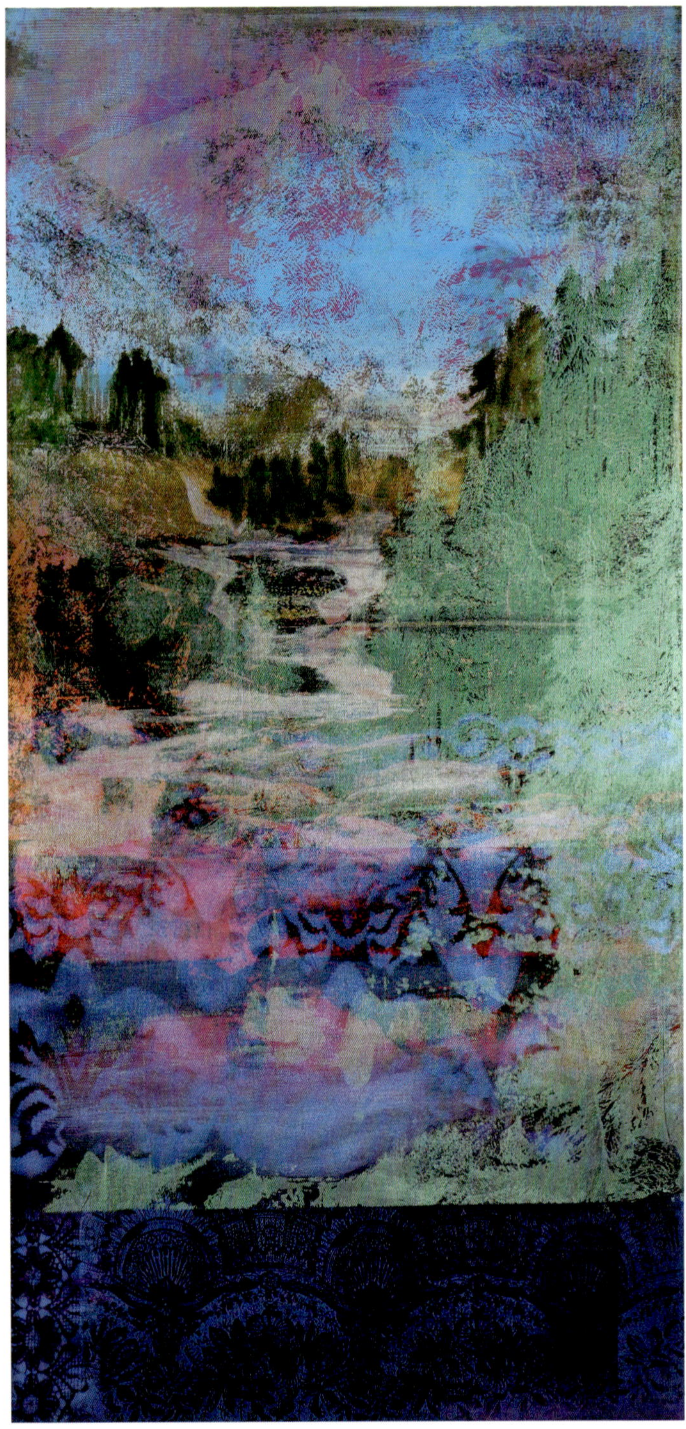

Rita Robillard
Time and Place

Essays by Bean Gilsdorf, Frances DeVuono,
Patricia Grieve Watkinson, and Linda Tesner

Hallie Ford Museum of Art
Willamette University
Salem, Oregon

Distributed by Oregon State University Press
Corvallis, Oregon

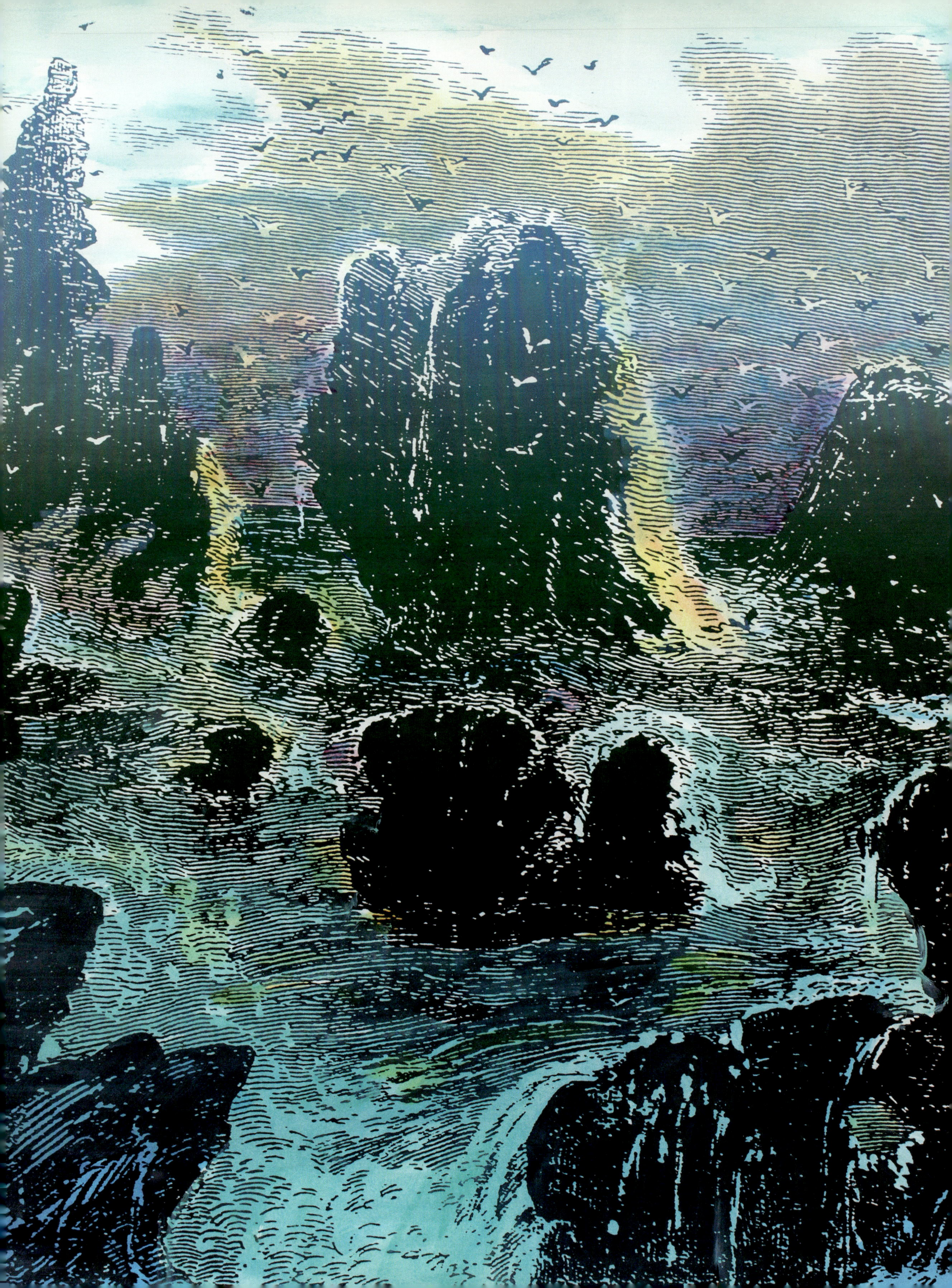

Contents

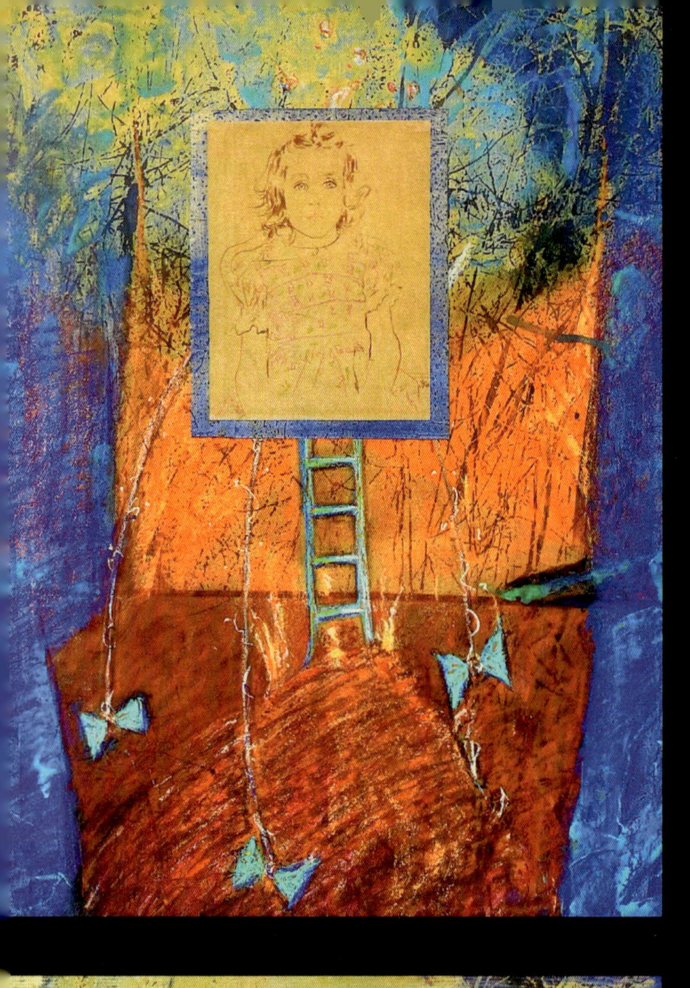
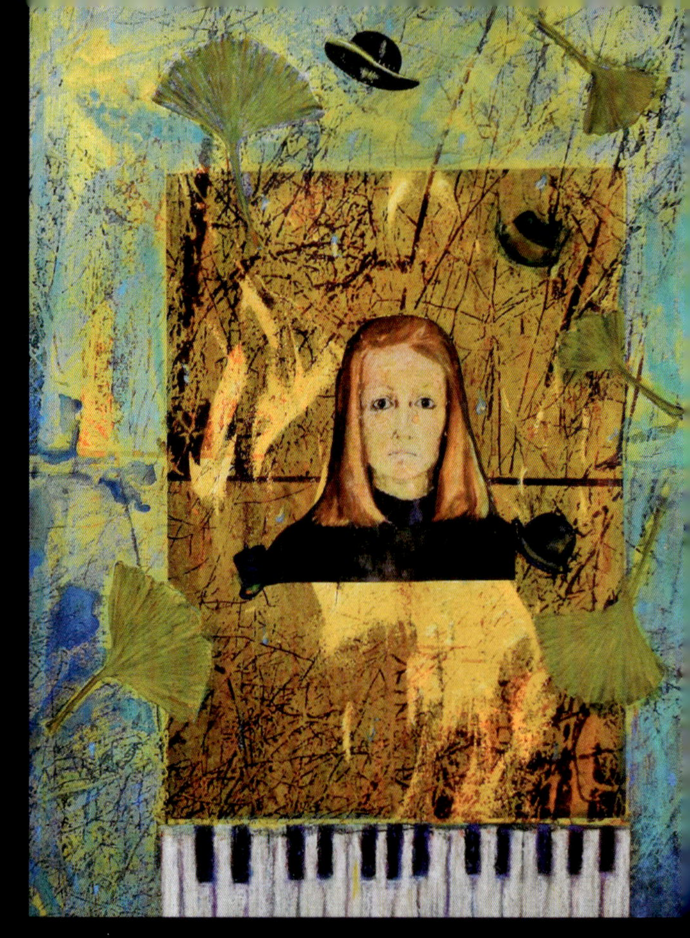
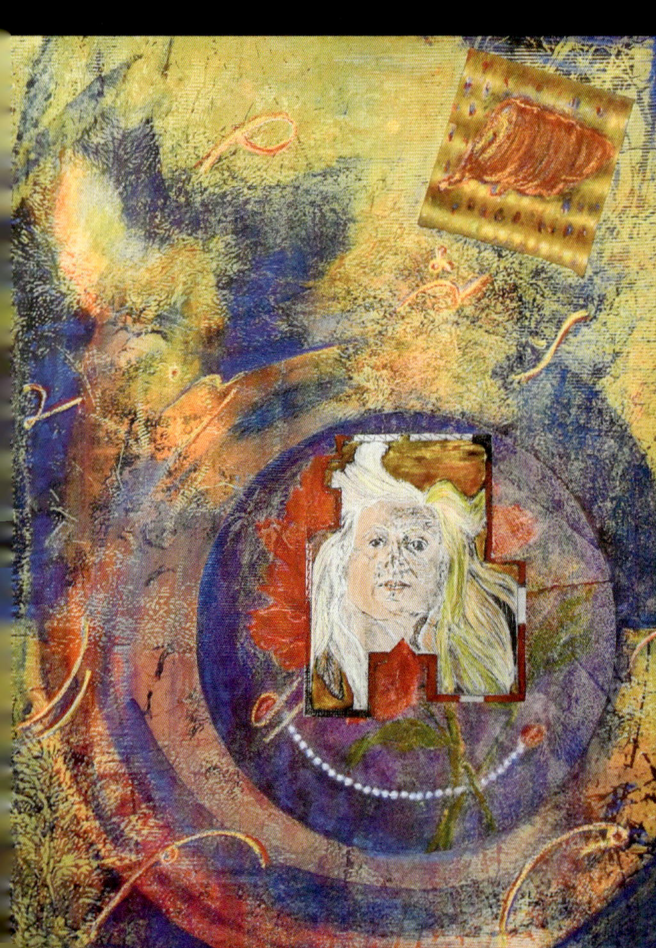
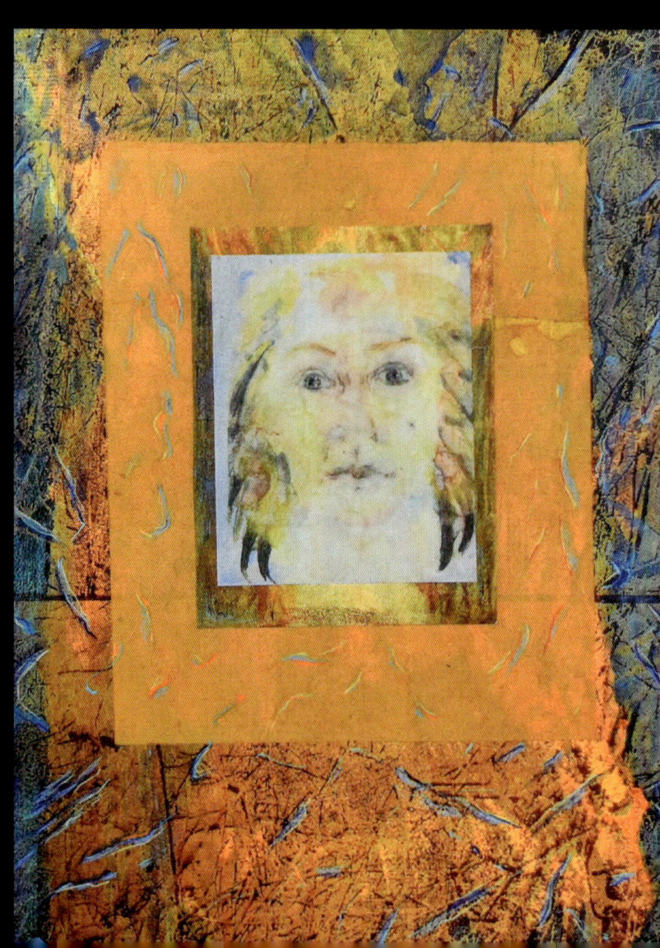

Preface

Rita Robillard (American, born 1944) is a highly regarded Portland, Oregon, mixed-media artist who explores themes of history, nature, ecology, and place in her work. A prolific printmaker and painter who is constantly pushing the boundaries of the printmaking medium, Robillard was born, raised, and educated in New York City, studied at Cooper Union in the early 1960s, lived and worked in Brazil in the early 1970s, and earned her BA degree, with honors, and her MFA degree at the University of California, Berkeley, in fine arts. A gifted and inspirational teacher, she was on the art faculties at the University of California, Davis, the San Francisco Art Institute, the Rhode Island School of Design, Washington State University in Pullman, and Portland State University, where she taught printmaking and chaired the art department.

Rita Robillard: Time and Place is the latest in an ongoing series of Hallie Ford Museum of Art exhibitions and books that are intended to chronicle and celebrate the art history of our region and is yet another example of our commitment to the art and artists of the Pacific Northwest. This is our thirty-fifth book published in twenty-two years, a monumental achievement for an institution of our size. Other regional artists featured in previous exhibitions and books include Rick Bartow, Frank Boyden (one exhibition, two books), Louis Bunce, Russell Childers, Richard Elliott, Joe Feddersen, Clifford Gleason, Carl Hall, Charles Heaney, Manuel Izquierdo, George Johanson, Mel Katz, Henk Pander, Lucinda Parker, Nelson Sandgren, Marie Watt, Harry Widman, and Jan Zach, among others.

On behalf of the faculty, staff, and students at Willamette University and myself, I would like to express my thanks and appreciation to a number of people without whose help this project would not have been possible. I would like to thank Bean Gilsdorf, Frances DeVuono, Patricia Grieve Watkinson, and Linda Tesner for writing thoughtful and insightful essays about different phases in the artist's life and career. I am further indebted to graphic designer Phil Kovacevich for his masterful design of the Rita Robillard book (our thirty-second book together); editor extraordinaire Nick Allison for his skillful copyediting of the various essays, biography, and photo captions; proofreader Carrie Wicks for reviewing Phil's page layouts; and photographers Katie Babb, Bill Bachhuber, Dan Kvitka, Paul Lee, Hart Monyatovsky, Dale Peterson, Paul Rich, and Brandon Sorg for their beautiful photography of Rita's work. In addition, I would like to thank Rita for sharing a number of photographs from her personal collection.

Self-Portraits, 2022, digital print on paper, 20 × 16 inches, collection of the artist.

Exhibitions like *Rita Robillard: Time and Place* would not be possible without the generosity of collectors, and I would like to thank the many collectors who agreed to loan their Rita Robillard works to the exhibition: the Jordan Schnitzer Museum of Art at Washington State University in Pullman; Ross Jory; Bruce Landrey and Michele DesMarais; Deborah and Martin Merkle; the Portland Art Museum in Portland, Oregon; Judith and David Rosner; Michael Rossman; and Freda Sherburne. Additionally, Rita would like to extend special thanks to Hallie Ford Museum of Art director John Olbrantz for curating the exhibition and overseeing the publication of the book; gallerist Bob Kochs of the Augen Gallery in Portland and his wife, Phyllis Osborne, as well as professor emerita Sue Taylor of Portland State University, for their ongoing friendship and professional support over the years; and Kate Babb and Hart Monyatovsky for their computer skills and technical support.

At the Hallie Ford Museum of Art, I would like to thank my dedicated, talented, and hardworking staff for their help with various aspects of the project: collections and exhibitions curator Jonathan Bucci; education curator Elizabeth Garrison; membership/public relations manager Andrea Foust; assistant to the director Jenny Stier; security officer Jason Lazafami; front desk receptionists Dana Eckfield and Leslie Whitaker; and custodian Maria Valdez. In addition, I want to express my thanks and appreciation to contract preparators Silas Cook and Fred Soelzer of Portland for their beautiful design and installation of the exhibition. At the Oregon State University Press, I would like to thank my friend and colleague Tom Booth, director of the press, for agreeing to distribute the Robillard book, our fourth book together.

The Hallie Ford Museum of Art would not have been able to organize the exhibition or publish the accompanying book without additional financial support, and I want to express my thanks and appreciation to the Ford Family Foundation for their ongoing commitment to Oregon art and artists; to several anonymous donors who provided gifts in support of our exhibitions and programs; to the late Maribeth Collins, who provided an endowment gift that generates funds for the Hallie Ford Museum of Art to organize exhibitions and publications that focus on Pacific Northwest art; to the *Oregonian*/Oregon Live for their advertising support; and to the City of Salem's Transient Occupancy Tax funds and the Oregon Arts Commission for their ongoing support of our exhibitions, programs, and related services. Finally, and by no means least, I would like to thank artist Rita Robillard for her help with the project over the past two years and for her warmth, passion, dedication, good humor, and commitment to excellence and innovation in printmaking and the other visual arts.

John Olbrantz
The Maribeth Collins Director

Queen of the Night I, from the series *Flower Serenade: A Gift of Time,* 2021, screenprint and oil on panel, 18 × 18 inches, courtesy of the artist and the Augen Gallery.

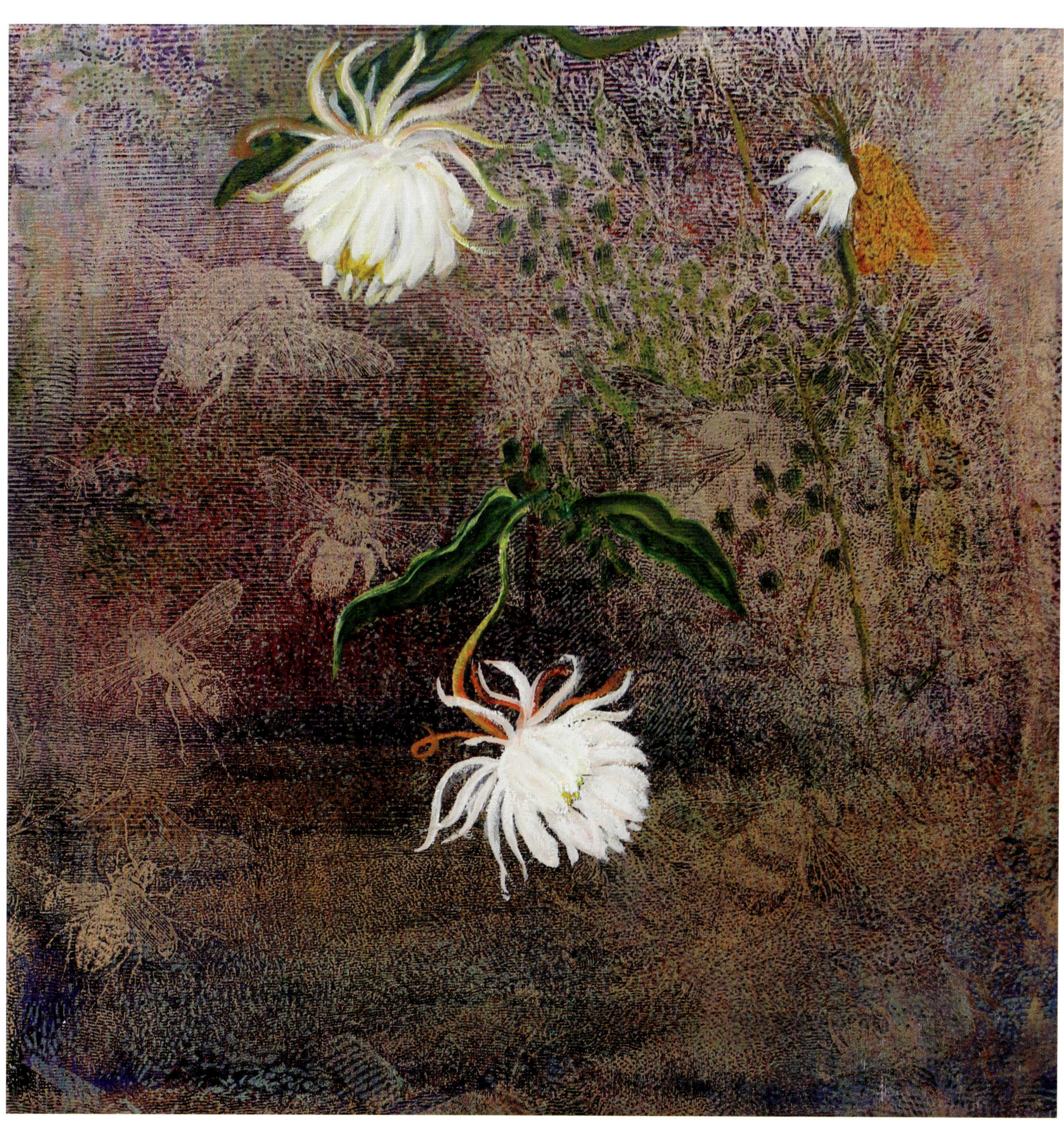

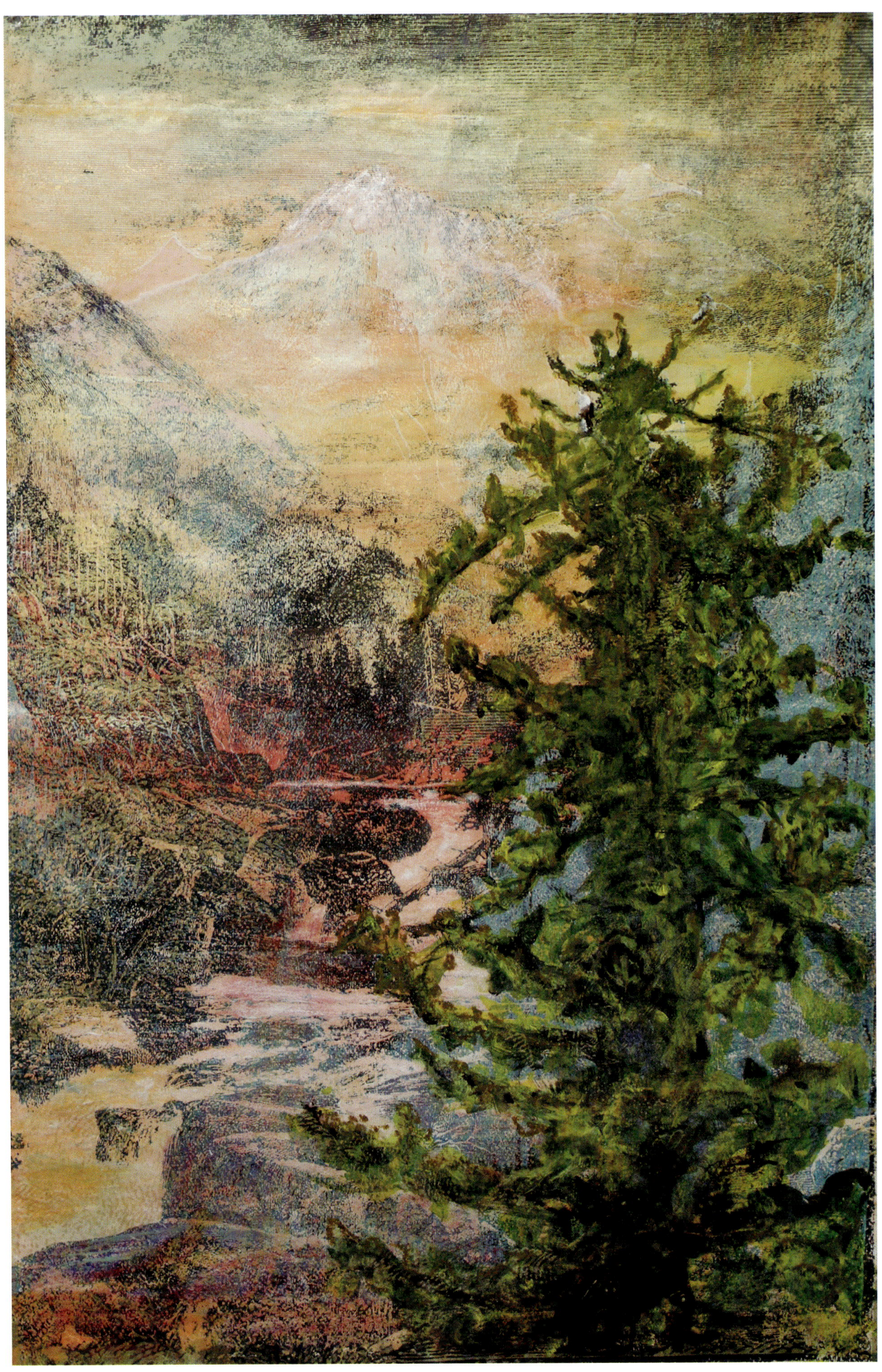

Parts of the Landscape:
The Career and Studio Practice of Rita Robillard

Bean Gilsdorf

Substrate (1944–1986)

If you have ever hiked to a summit in the North American West, you have likely glimpsed a similar view: From where you stand, a lone conifer near the peak rises up from a slowly dispersing haze. Below you, the landscape stretches away in rough outlines of hill and valley; the burbling, hissing river you passed on your way up is now a thin, silent thread, drawing your eye along its passage through the forest. On the far side of the valley, a snowcapped peak hovers like an apparition. Its spectral presence makes the tree in front of you seem even more vibrantly alive, its heavy boughs lifting slightly as its upper trunk sways in the breeze now whispering into your ears. Look closely and you'll spy a raptor in the topmost branches, shifting its weight from side to side as it seeks a firmer grip.

Such is the experience conjured in my mind by Rita Robillard's *Nesting* (2021), a mixed-media work of screenprint, acrylic, and drawing on gampi paper, part of her *Flower Seranade: A Gift of Time* series (fig. 1). These works transmit the sense-memory of scenes like the one I've just described, re-immersing me in the experience. In *Nesting*, Robillard uses line, form, texture, color, and scale to evoke an experiential state rather than a merely visual tableau. In her most recent artist statement, she writes, "The compelling questions in my work are about place, both the external environment of various places and my place within them. How does place affect our values, and differ from urban and rural and eastern and western vantage points?"[1]

Such questions articulate the foundational concepts behind the artist's work, which merges the physical and psychological characteristics of environmental forms. Robillard has been living and working in the Pacific Northwest since 1986, but her emotional and intellectual engagement with the biosphere—and the issues that arise from the human presence within it—began when she was a child. Born in 1944 in New York City, she grew up with access to Gramercy Park's famous gated garden, an oasis within the surrounding landscape of brick and concrete. The calm, lush refuge of the park is magnified in her early memories against an ominous backdrop of air-raid drills and elementary-school "duck and cover" protocols that served as constant reminders of the threat of nuclear destruction. Over the course of Robillard's artistic career, this juxtaposition of natural sanctuary with man-made jeopardy would eventually develop into a theme explored through many bodies of work.

Fig. 1: *Nesting*, from the series *Flower Serenade: A Gift of Time*, 2021, screenprint, acrylic, oil pastel, and colored pencil on gampi paper, 33 × 22 inches, courtesy of the artist and the Augen Gallery.

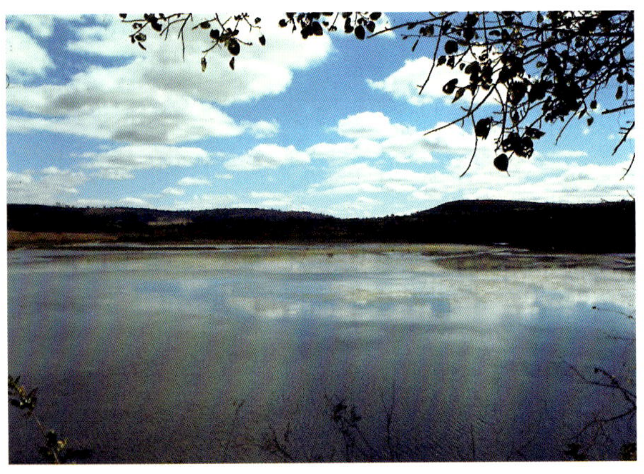

A view of Lake Sumidouro, the inspiration for the series *Spirit Ground*, located in the state of Minas Gerais, Brazil, 1973.

Starting out as a young artist, however, she was most influenced by her immediate cultural environment. Robillard attended art classes in 1962 at New York's Cooper Union, where her early paintings nodded to Abstract Expressionism and Pop Art as she worked toward finding an expression of her own concerns and interests. After graduating from Cooper Union in 1966, she moved west to California with her husband and her daughter, Danielle, ushering in a decade of periodic itinerancy that would prove to be important to her aesthetic and cultural development as an artist. The family resided first in Hollywood in 1968, where her second daughter, Rana, was born. They then decamped briefly to San Francisco before departing for São Paulo and rural Brazil, where she taught art to young children from 1971 to 1974. When the family returned to California in 1974, they moved first to Concord and then to Lafayette before finally settling in Berkeley. Facets of these landscapes would come to play a role in Robillard's artistic practice. In 1977, she enrolled as an undergraduate in the art department at the University of California at Berkeley, completing the work for her BA with honors in 1979 with a focus on printmaking, and then going directly into the MFA program the following fall.

At Berkeley, Robillard minored in Asian art history. The influence of her studies can be felt in works like *Nesting*, whose composition seems to follow the precepts of *shan shui*–style landscapes. These are always defined by three components: first, a path that leads the eye into the distance; then, a threshold such as a mountain; and finally, the heart or focal point of the composition. *Shan shui* paintings also value phenomenological experience and emotional interpretation over a visually predetermined realism. At the end of her four-year period of intense study and experimentation, Robillard expressed a similar ethos in her 1981 MFA thesis statement, which accompanied a body of abstract etchings on mulberry paper (figs. 2, 3, 4): "I want to communicate a passion for beauty and the survival for humanity."[2]

Education and service have always been important components of Robillard's career. While still in her graduate program, in 1979, Robillard began a teaching practice that would prove to be foundational to the development of her studio work. Like many artists', her first positions were peripatetic: she was employed for two terms at University of California at Davis, then for a year at the San Francisco Art Institute, and then another year at Chabot College in Livermore. In all, these appointments enabled her to make connections in her field and participate in conversations that would help shape the discipline. In 1981, she initiated what would become a lifetime of administrative service to the profession when she accepted a two-year term as a board member for the California Society of Printmakers. In time, she would

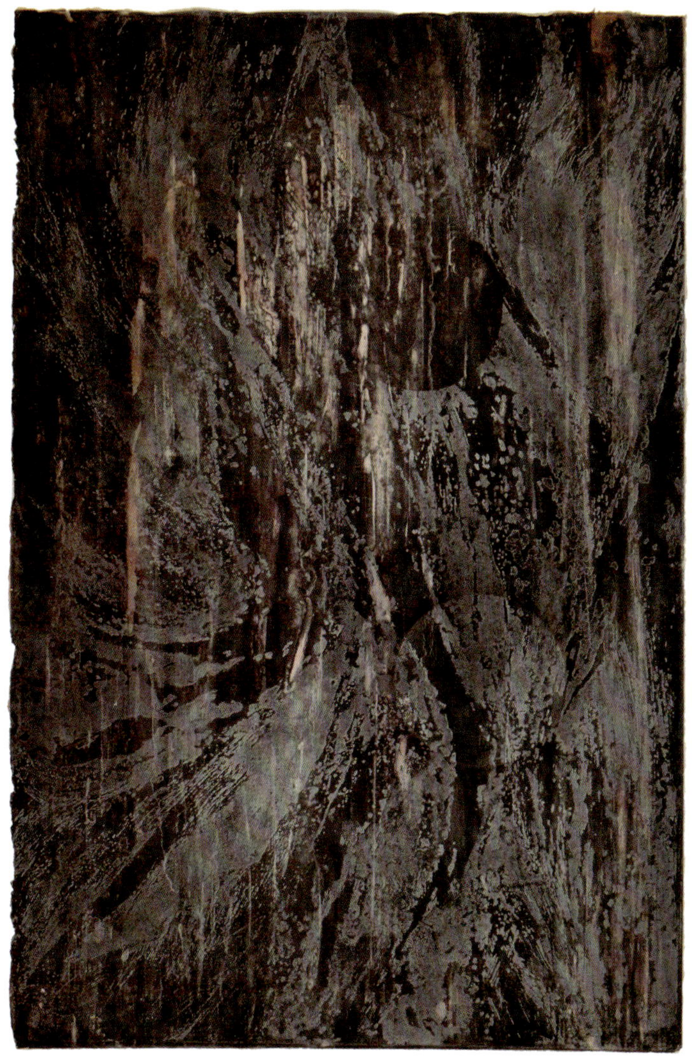

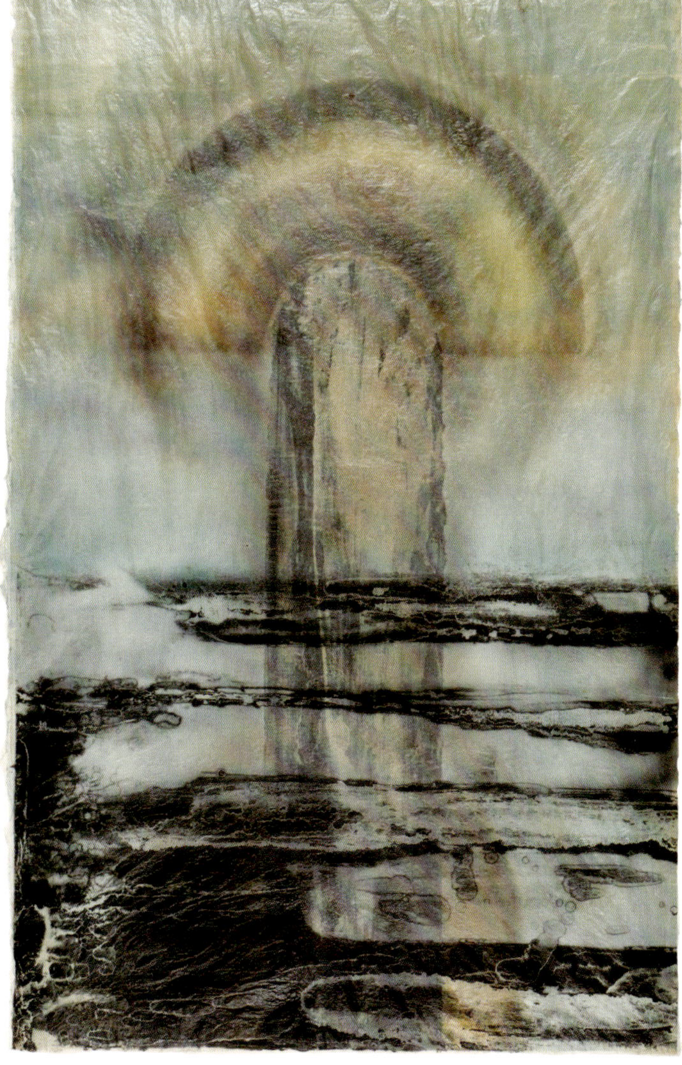

Fig. 2: *Double Eclipse*, from the series *Spirit Ground*, 1980, etching on mulberry paper, 35¾ × 24 inches, collection of the artist.

Fig. 3: *Heroes in the Seaweed*, from the series *Spirit Ground*, 1980, etching on mulberry paper mounted on cotton paper, 35 × 23¾ inches, collection of the artist.

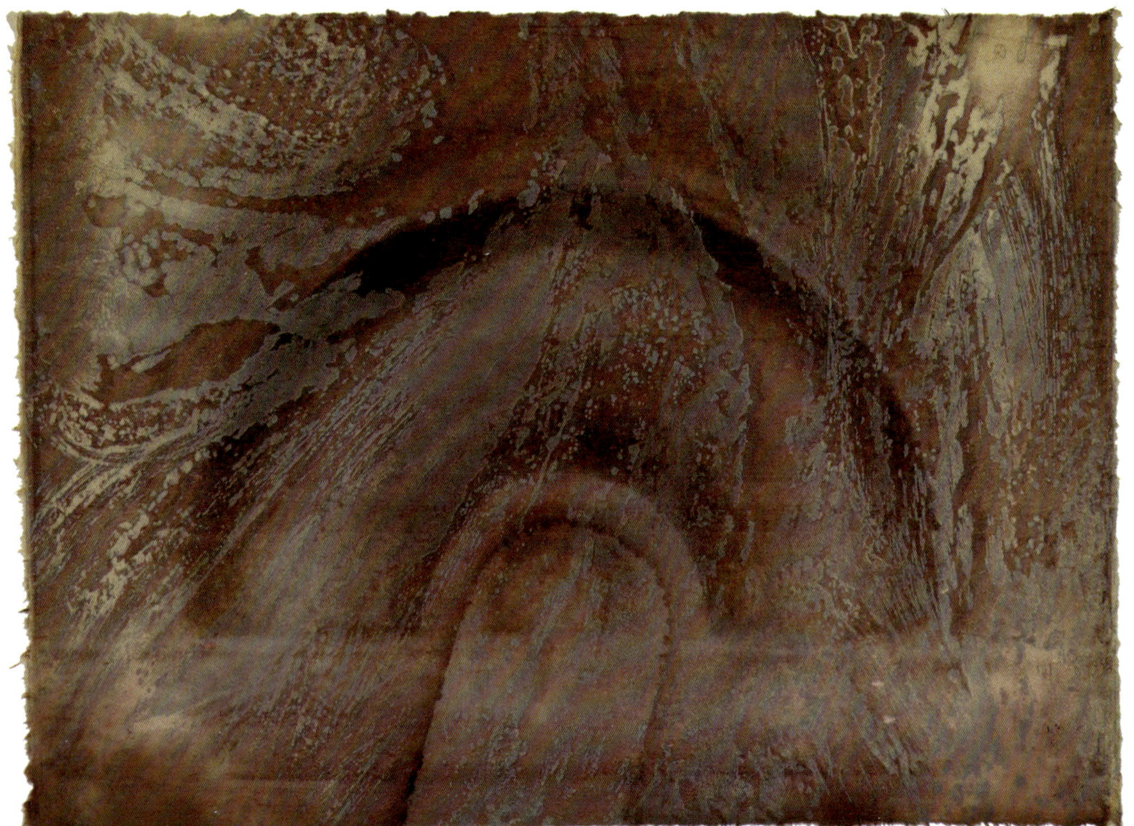

go on to serve in prominent positions as a regional conference chair for the Northwest Print
Council, as a board member for the Women's Caucus for Art, and as the chair of the Visual
Arts Committee of the College Art Association, among others.

In 1986, Robillard relocated to Pullman, Washington, to join the faculty of the fine arts
department at Washington State University as an assistant professor. Eventually becoming
a full professor, she credits the stability that this position provided as crucial to supporting
her exploratory practice: "Being on the faculty, I didn't have to be famous. That gave me a lot
of freedom."[3] This professional liberty also enabled her to upgrade the educational processes
and materials that the academic staff and students were using at WSU. In 1987, Robillard
was awarded a $10,000 grant to replace the acid baths and toxic solvents in the printmaking
area with environmentally friendly water-based inks, a prescient switch that anticipated the
late-twentieth-century resurgence in "green" practices intended to reduce harmful exposure to
substances that damage both humans and nature.

Background (1987–1998)

After the frequent relocations and job changes that shaped Robillard's experience in the 1970s
and early '80s, the work she produced in Pullman expresses a strengthening—a rooting—
of her practice. The environmental writer Barry Lopez has noted that the desire to dwell

spiritually as well as physically in a region "requires not only time but a kind of local expertise, and intimacy with place that few of us ever develop."[4] In Eastern Washington, Robillard was surrounded by protected vistas: the Umatilla, Wallowa-Whitman, and Malheur National Forests to the south in Oregon; the Boise, Salmon-Challis, and Idaho Panhandle National Forests to the east in Idaho; and the Kootenai, Colville, and Okanogan-Wenatchee National Forests to the north in Idaho and Washington—to say nothing of the Yakima, Colville, Coeur d'Alene, Nez Perce, and Umatilla Reservations that encircle the area. In the twelve years Robillard spent at Washington State University, it seems only natural that the work she produced grew ever more reflective of the environmental forms that abound in the wild areas of the Pacific Northwest. In her hybrid paintings and prints from the late 1980s and early 1990s, Robillard was developing that essence of inhabiting a place and absorbing its history.

Take 1987's *Night View* from the series *Thicket/Threshold*, a sixty-by-seventy-inch semi-abstracted landscape depicted at night, with a dark-blue background and greenish-black lines that resolve into a stand of trees, as moonlight paints the foreground in patches of shimmering light (fig. 5). This observation of natural forms from deep within night-darkened woods could serve as a reminder of the region's most pressing environmental controversies from that period: clear-cutting, erosion, tree sitting, "eco-terrorism," endangered species protection—all the issues adjacent to the old-growth logging industry that divided communities, both rural and urban, into political factions.

Nationwide, the forests of the Pacific Northwest became a symbol on which to construct cultural frameworks for understanding our present and future. Though she has never called herself an activist, many of Robillard's bodies of work evoke the nobility of her subjects, an orientation that seems aligned with conservation and preservation. From 1991 to 1993, she created the series *Cottonwoods of the Palouse*, inspired by Chinese sixteenth- and seventeenth-century scrolls, and based on drawings of deciduous black cottonwood trees that are native to the western states, whose trunks grow to a massive diameter of six feet (fig. 6). In Robillard's mulberry-paper-on-Tyvek scrolls, the trees' power is felt in the way their rough, dark trunks wend forcefully skyward against a backdrop of clear blue. The trees were "drawn from direct observation, and processed into a flat image,"[5] Robillard told me—a sentence that is not only a fact about the artworks' creation but potentially also a metaphor for the ways in which the wild, extant landscape is sometimes flattened into political allegory that defines the western states, turning a vibrantly palpable ecosystem into an idealized abstraction that has been used to symbolize everything from harmony with nature to cultural and territorial dominance.

Other types of landscapes further shaped Robillard's artistic concepts: Around that same time, she produced the series *Votives for Hanford*, a suite of screenprinted and collaged works that combine images of forests with scientific diagrams of isotopes and religious iconography (fig. 7). The series examines the problem of nuclear waste from the decommissioned Cold

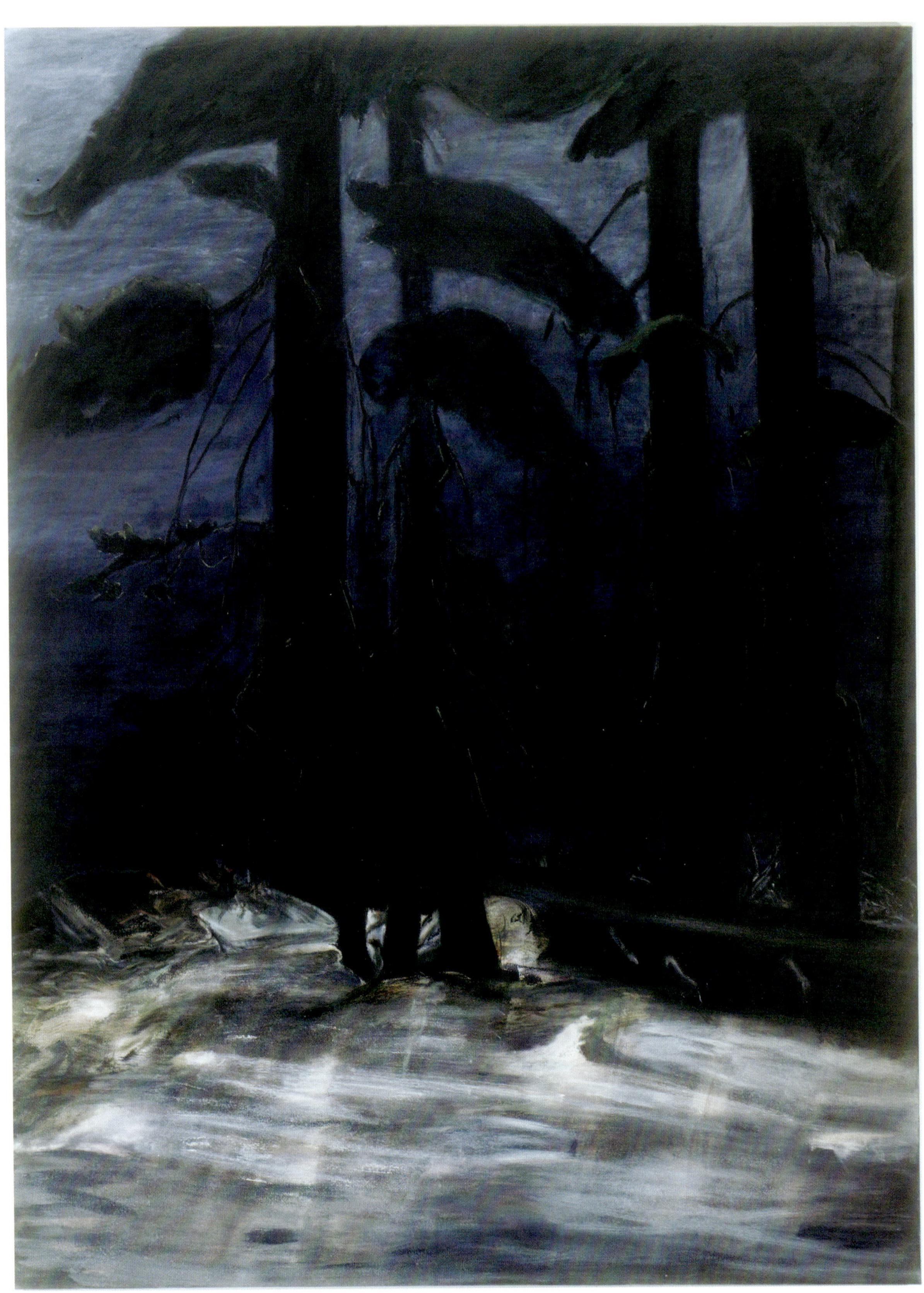

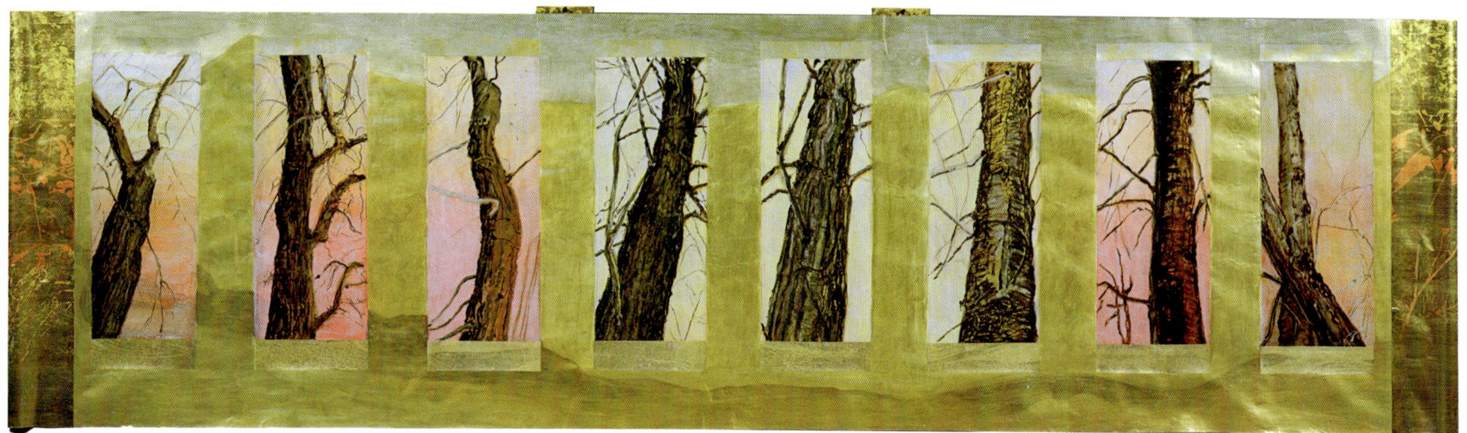

Fig. 5: *Night View*, from the series *Thicket/Threshold*, 1987, oil on canvas, 72 × 60 inches, collection of the artist.

Fig. 6: *Cottonwoods of the Palouse*, 1993–95, screenprint, acrylic, and oil sticks on gampi or mulberry paper mounted on Tyvek, 36 × 120 inches, collection of the Jordan Schnitzer Museum of Art, Washington State University, Pullman, gift of the artist in honor of Pat and Sam Smith, 2015.10.1.

Fig. 7: *Hark in the Forest*, from the series *Votives for Hanford*, 1990–96, revised in 2019–20, pigment print mounted on panel, 20 × 16 inches, courtesy of the artist and the Augen Gallery.

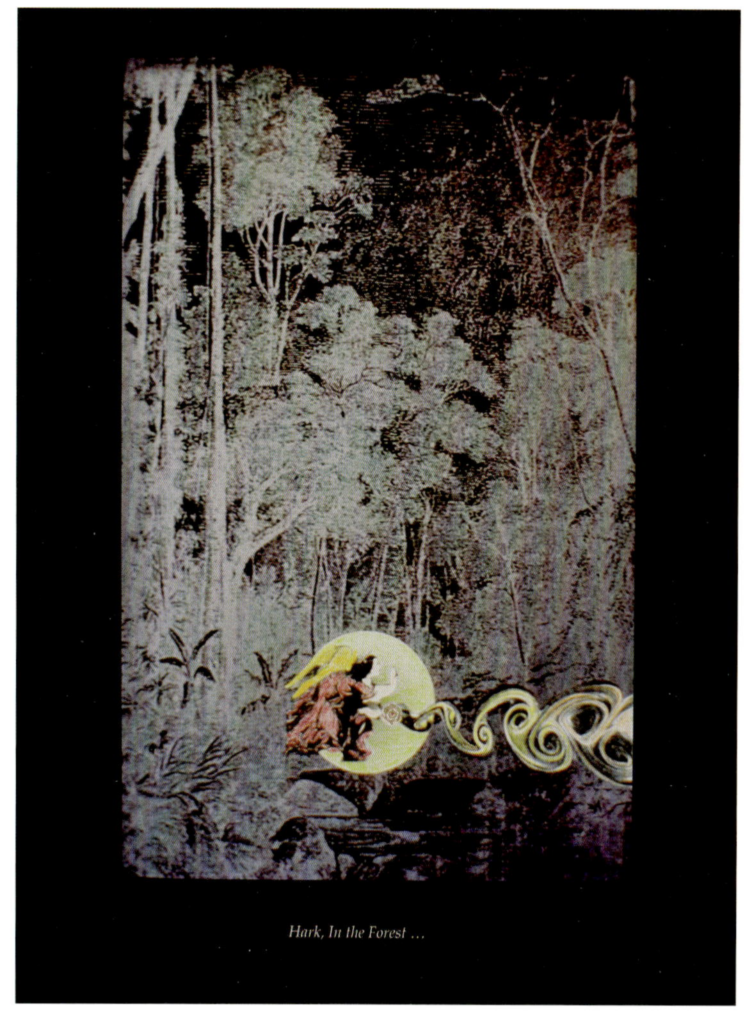

War–era nuclear facility in Hanford, Washington, which subsequently contaminated the surrounding environment. Selections from the *Votives for Hanford* series were included in exhibitions and conference panels throughout that decade, most notably in the 1993 exhibition *Yes, in My Back Yard?* at the Allied Arts Gallery in Richland, Washington. A brochure from the gallery explains that the works in the exhibition were brought together to create "a forum where diverse points of view can meet" to foster a conversation around "the nuclear debate."[6] Three decades later, Robillard's own statement that "the scope and reality of the problem lie outside human comprehension"[7] has been borne out: Hanford remains the most contaminated nuclear site in the United States, with radioactive waste leaks reported as recently as April 2021.

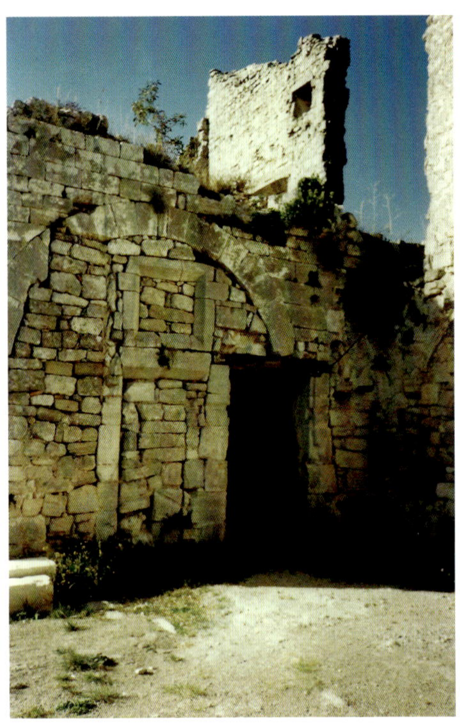

A wall from the ruined château of the Marquis de Sade, Lacoste, France, 1992.

In her travels outside the region, Robillard continued to observe and record her experience of the landscape; when she returned, she incorporated those encounters into bodies of work that nevertheless depict the Pacific Northwest in highly interpretive fashion. For example, in 1992 and 1993, Robillard attended two residencies that would shape her future work. First, she spent four months in southern France as an artist-in-residence in Lacoste, a medieval village near the caves of Lascaux, where early artists—probably women—decorated the cave walls and ceilings with handprints and animal drawings. Robillard was inspired by these ancient forms and by the crumbling walls of the village; she also visited the panopticon in the hilltop château of the Marquis de Sade. The following year, echoing her experience in France, she spent many weekends in a Forest Service fire lookout tower in North Idaho. These towers—tall, spare platforms that allow watchers to spot distant fires—were once a crucial part of environmental management, but as their official uses dwindled, they became available to the general public for short stays. Up in her tower, the artist was able to see for miles across the treetops, taking photographs of sunsets and sunrises, thinking about human surveillance within the wilderness.

These two experiences fed her 1993–94 project *Lookout/Outlook*, an installation that debuted at Washington State University (fig. 8). The work is "a 360-degree view of human projections and reflections on the natural world,"[8] the artist told me. To make this work, Robillard digitally manipulated her photographs of sunsets and sunrises to look like fires and printed them on thin gampi paper. She glued the prints to a thirty-six-inch-high band of Tyvek that had been screenprinted with images of the medieval walls from the Lacoste residency.

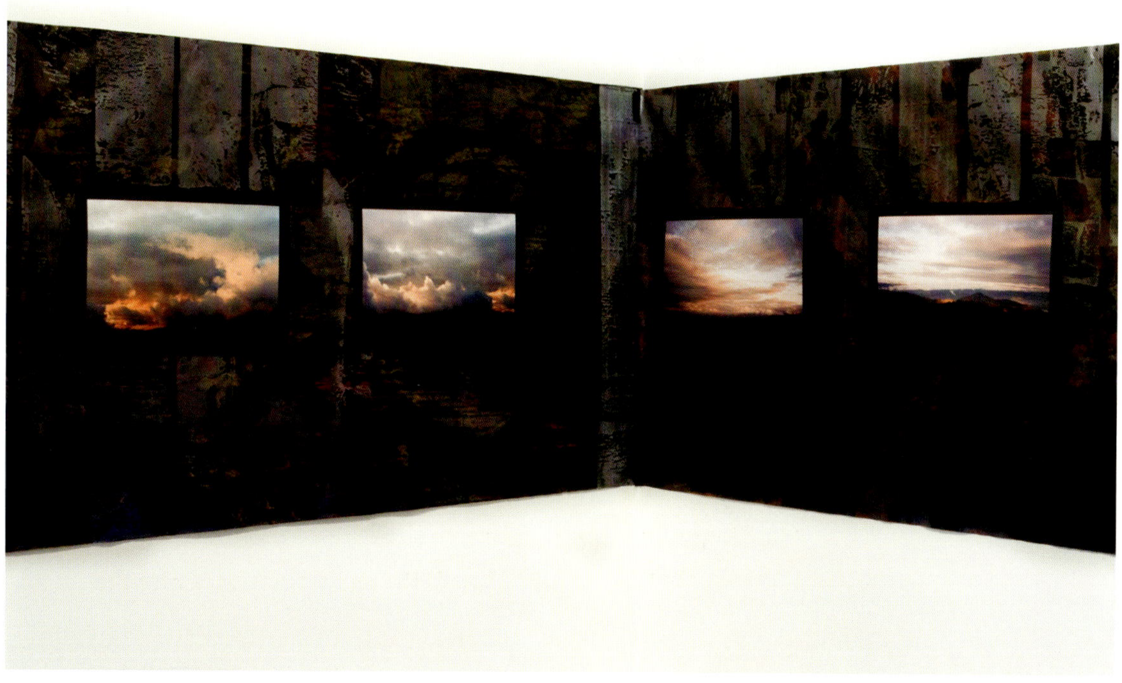

The result is a work that speaks to the ecological history of the Pacific Northwest and gives the viewer a sense of looking out the windows of a fortress onto a massive, encompassing forest fire. *Lookout/Outlook* was exhibited again in 2009 at the Littman Gallery at Portland State University, where viewers were given the opportunity to engage with ever-changing landscapes, both within and without.

In evoking the terrifying power and vast destruction of a forest fire—now an all-too-common occurrence in western North America—*Lookout/Outlook* points to the sublime. It could also perhaps stand as an example of what Chinese American geographer Yi-Fu Tuan, writing in an essay entitled "Thought and Landscape: The Eye and the Mind's Eye," considers "the side view":

> Landscape is an ordering of reality from different angles. The vertical view sees landscape as a domain, a work unit, or a natural system necessary to human livelihood. . . . The side view, in contrast is personal, moral, and aesthetic. A person is *in* the landscape [. . . looking . . .] from a particular spot and not from an abstract point in space. . . . Landscape appears to us through an effort of the imagination exercised over a highly selective array of sense data.[9]

In other words, the interpretations of the artist are unmistakable in the creation of these views, a merging of authorial vision with an affective understanding of place; this combination produces a subjective and experiential description, a perspective with the potential to demand new ways of seeing place that stimulates a novel response in the viewer.

Middle Ground (1998–2012)

Robillard's work and career continued to evolve within the context of the Pacific Northwest. In 1998, the artist moved to Portland, Oregon, to join the faculty in the department of art at Portland State University, where she taught drawing and mixed-media classes and conducted graduate seminars in professional practices. From 1998 to 2001, Robillard held the position of department chair, and subsequently was MFA chair from 2005 to 2007. In 2006, her second year as MFA chair, she won PSU's Teaching Excellence Award. From 2003 to 2008 she served as the vice president and program chair of the Graphic Arts Council of the Portland Art Museum.

The work she produced during this time extended and refined Robillard's practice of layering imagery, and the architectural environment of the surrounding city entered into her work. Her 2001 solo exhibition *Time and Place* at Elizabeth Leach Gallery in Portland displayed a suite of panels that combined screenprints made from nineteenth-century landscape etchings found in historical archives with the artist's own digital photographs taken in the metro area. In each panel, the modern digital image is superimposed on the archaic lines of the landscape: a carp photographed at Portland's refined Japanese garden sits on top of a riverside wilderness in *Gardens and Vistas* (fig. 9); rivet-laden girders atop an engraving of trees in *Steel* (fig. 10); or the concrete mass of a bridge's abutment centered atop a forest in *The Bridge* (fig. 11). Reviewing the exhibition for *Art in America* in 2002, the art historian Sue Taylor wrote, "The juxtaposition of these two images creates myriad contrasts: now/then, artifice/wilderness, alien/native, East/West. Robillard exploited the rich possibilities of this strategy . . . in tondos that float on scenes of Oregon as it was encountered by explorers and pioneers."[10] Adding to this sense of examination of the region's present and storied past, Taylor notes that the circular photographs "evoke the camera's lens, which organizes modern experience in a way unknown to Lewis and Clark."[11]

In a conversation in her studio, the artist told me, "Our experience of place affects who we become."[12] In this she echoes the sentiments of conservationist and philosopher Aldo Leopold, who formulated a "land ethic,"[13] a moral code based on the theory that relationships between humans and land are intertwined, and that care for people cannot be separated from care for the land. Leopold postulates that the key to extending a person's ethics beyond self-interest lies in direct contact with the natural world, and that the formation and retention of environmental values extend directly from this contact. Like the ethos of *shan shui* landscape paintings and Yi-Fu Tuan's "side view," this assumes an affective as well as an intellectual

Fig. 9: *Gardens and Vistas*, from the series *Time and Place*, 2001, screenprint and digital print on panel, 20 × 20 inches, private collection.

Fig. 10: *Steel*, from the series *Time and Place*, 2001, screenprint and digital print on panel, 20 × 20 inches, Regional Arts and Culture Visual Chronicles of Portland collection.

Fig. 11: *The Bridge*, from the series *Time and Place*, 2001, screenprint and digital print on panel, 20 × 20 inches, collection of Linda Wysong.

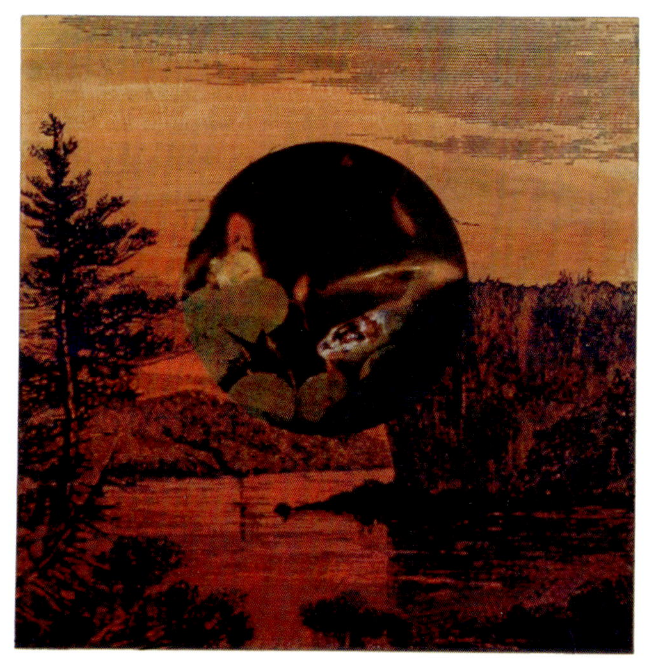

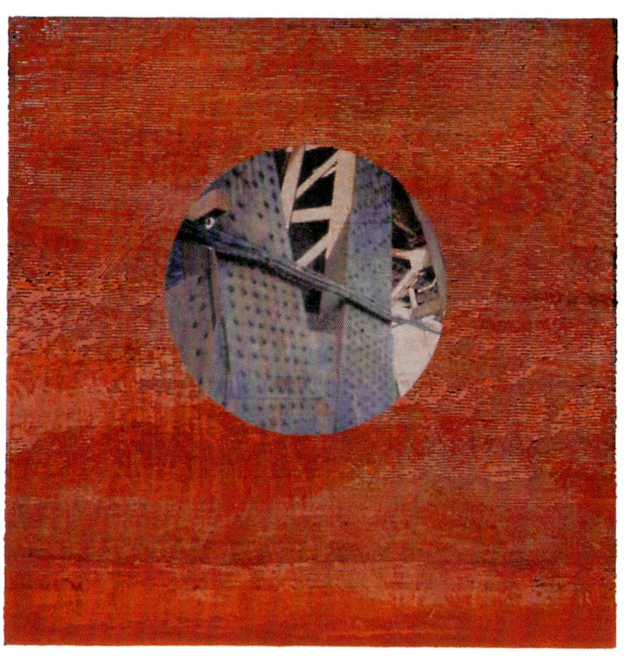

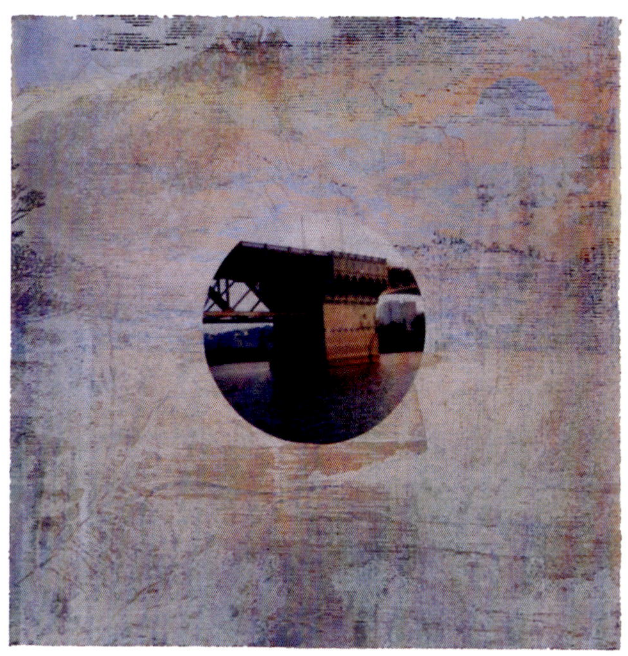

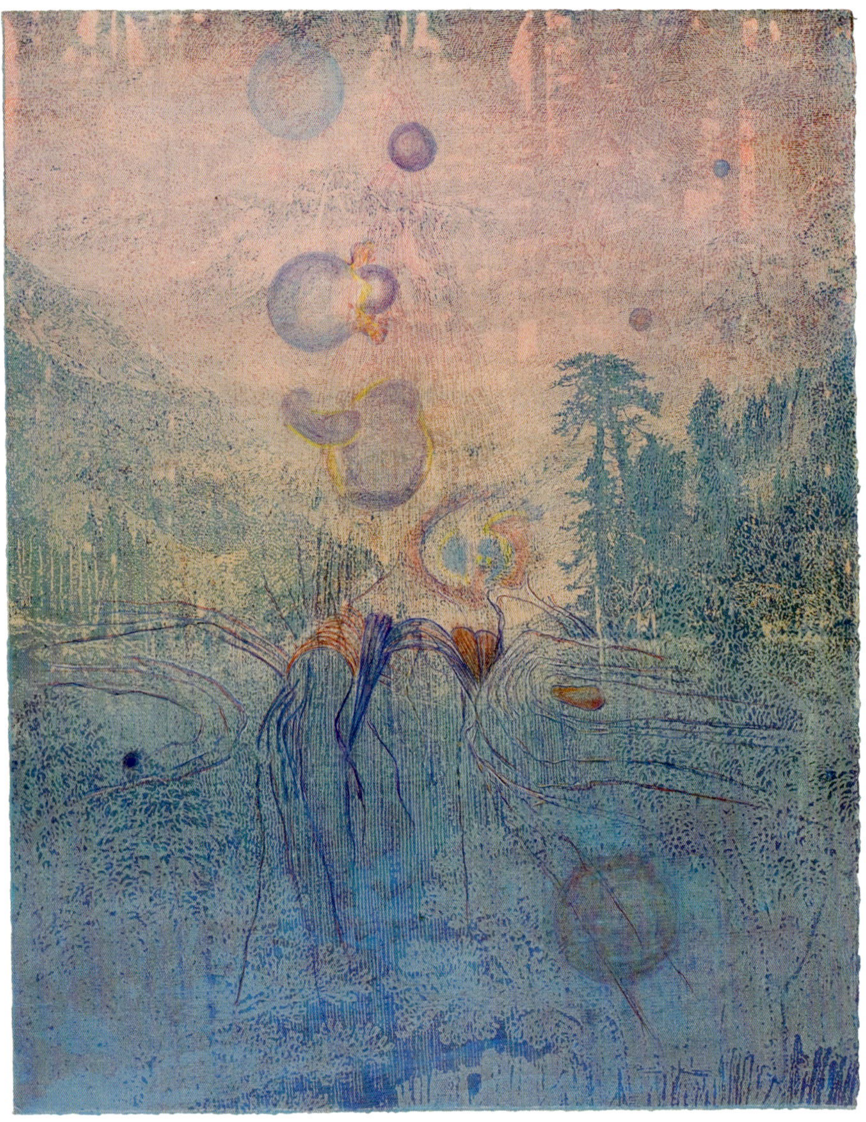

orientation; that to be present in the natural landscape—or to see it in a work of art, as a proxy—is to anchor one's attention in the metaphysical bond between self and surroundings.

The motif of the circle appears again in the biomorphic forms of *Luminous Frontiers*, a 2007 body of mixed-media works that combine screenprints and drawings on paper (fig. 12). Using iridescent inks and colored pencils, Robillard layered imagery of romantic vistas with celestial bodies inspired by images captured by the lens of the Hubble telescope: the spheres of faraway planets, globular nebulae, and swirling galaxies. The series brings together these terrestrial and extraterrestrial forms, and the title invokes both the limits of our own planet and of human expansion into space (fig. 13). Eight of these works were exhibited in *Place in Time* at the Ruth Chandler Williamson Gallery at Scripps College, and in a catalog essay for the exhibition, Sue Taylor calls the work "poetical cosmology."[14]

Concurrently with the fourteen-year span of her instructional and administrative duties at PSU, Robillard exhibited her work frequently in notable galleries such as A.I.R. Gallery in

Fig. 12: *Collisions in Time*, from the series *Luminous Frontiers*, 2007, screenprint and colored pencil on paper, 24½ × 20 inches, courtesy of the artist and the Augen Gallery.

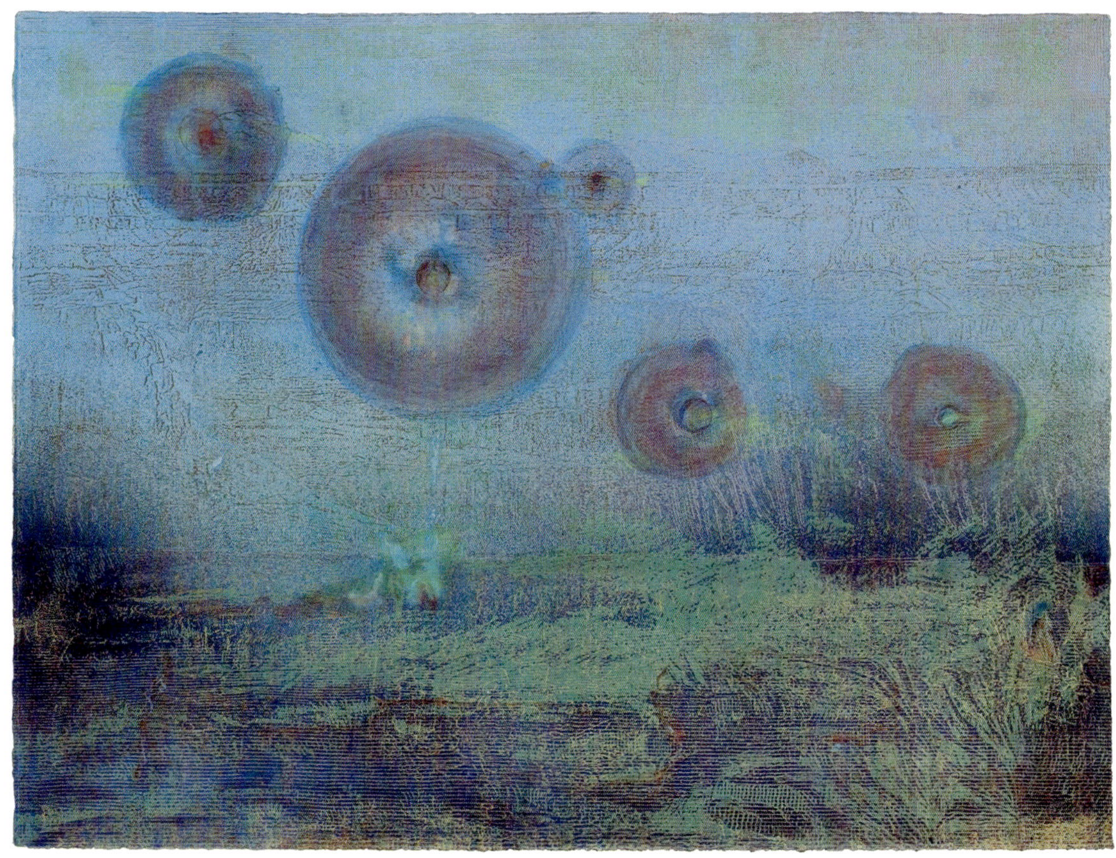

New York, Portland Institute for Contemporary Art, the Arts Center in Saratoga Springs, Lorinda Knight Gallery, and Augen Gallery. She also participated in the US Department of State's Art in Embassies program, which placed her work in embassies in Cameroon and Papua New Guinea. Robillard's work during this period was additionally supported by grants and awards from the Oregon Arts Commission, the College Art Association, and the Ford Family Foundation, among others, underwriting her projects and enabling the refinement of her oeuvre.

In 2011, Robillard attended a three-month residency at the Sitka Center for Art and Ecology on the coast of Oregon. It was here that she further explored the connections between art and science by working alongside a group of researchers who were studying the nearby Cascade Head Experimental Forest, a tract of land set aside in 1934 for the application of forestry techniques and the study of their impacts on the surrounding ecosystem. As a result of this residency, Robillard produced the works in what would become the series *And Then Again: Rifts on the Forest and Time*, medium- and large-format depictions of the tree species that are native to the region (figs. 14, 15). The largest of the artworks is *Coastal Range*, a six-panel view of a dense stand of conifers in hues that range from chartreuse to deep blue-green (front/back cover, fig. 16). The grouping of trees rises serenely in front of a grid made from gold acrylic paint whose tones shift depending on the angle of the viewer. The metallic gold background enhances the sense of royalty of the stand. In a statement for the work, the artist wrote that the series "evokes Eastern and Western pictorial traditions, and deliberately juxtaposes

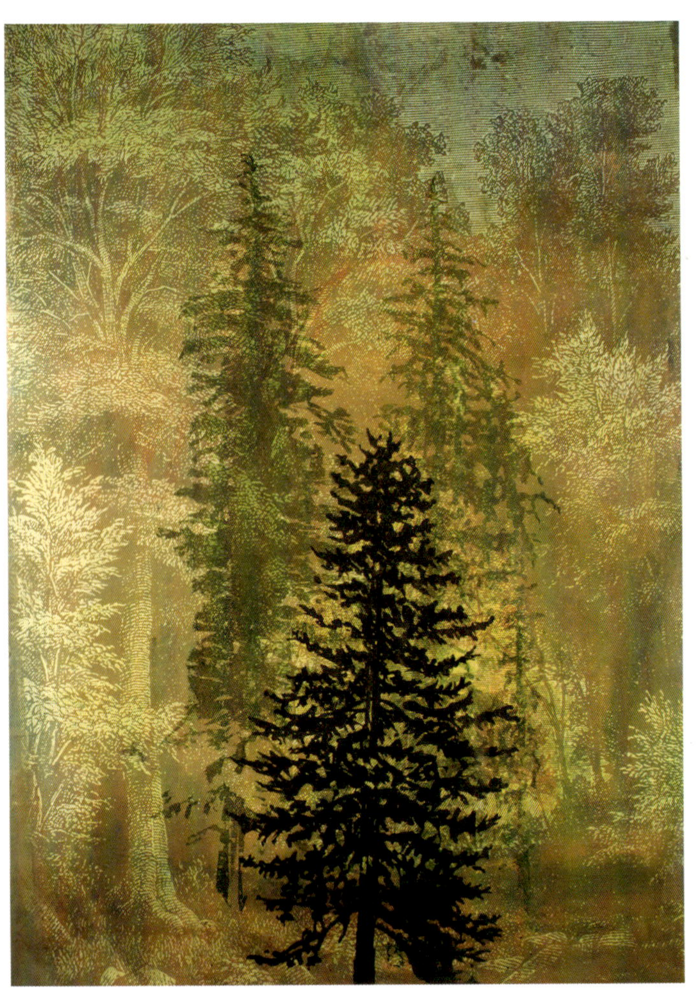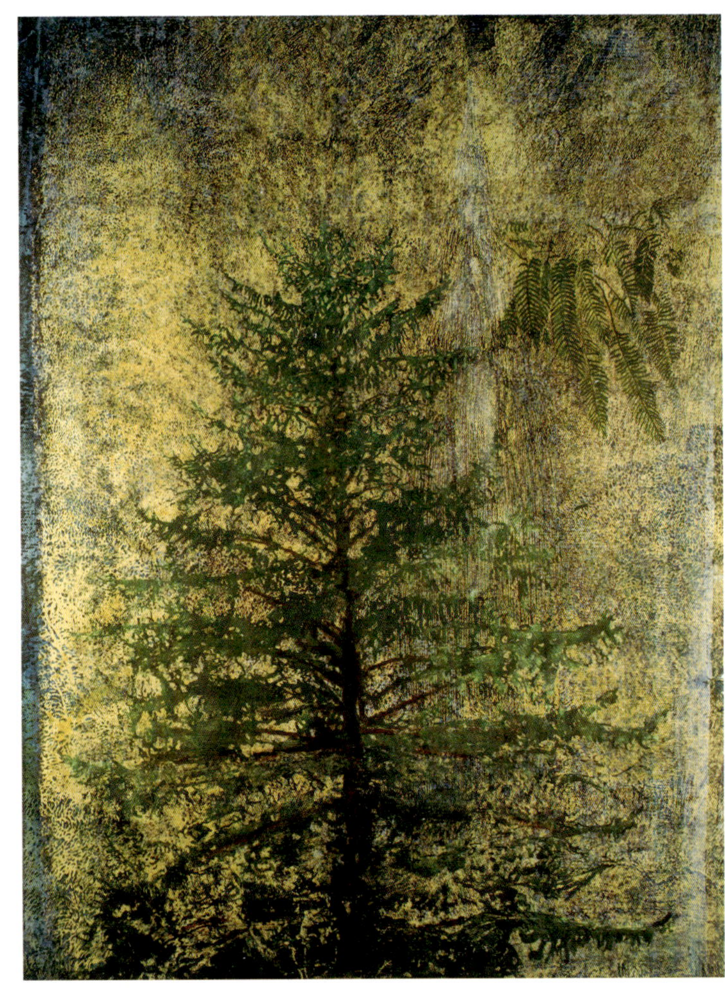

Fig. 14: *Sylvan Memoir*, from the series *And Then Again: Rifts on the Forest and Time*, 2012, screenprint and acrylic on Asian paper mounted on panel, 35 × 25½ inches, collection of Michael Rossman.

Fig. 15: *Temperate*, from the series *And Then Again: Rifts on the Forest and Time*, 2012, screenprint on mulberry paper, 33 × 23 inches, collection of Bruce Landrey and Michele DesMarais.

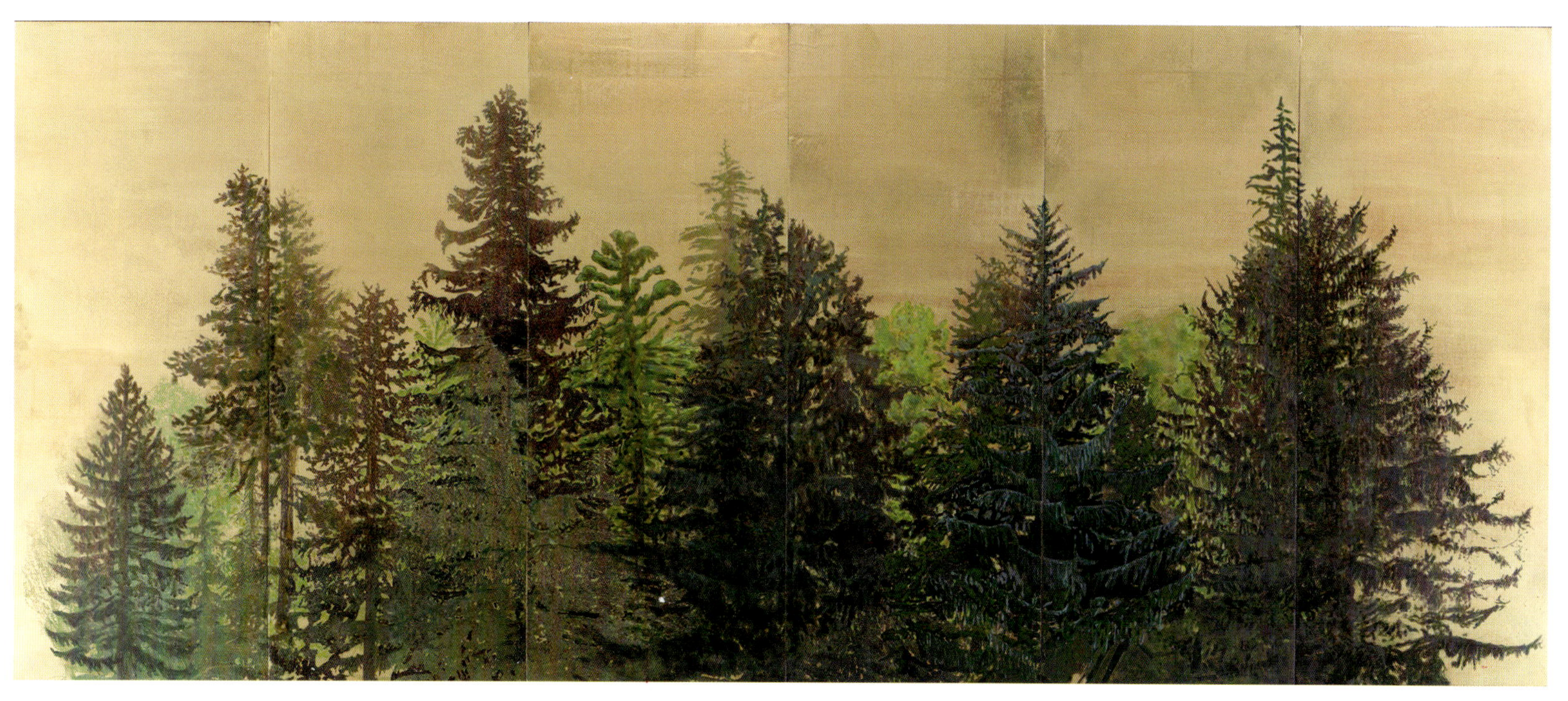

Fig. 16: *Coastal Range*, from the series *And Then Again: Rifts on the Forest and Time*, 2012, screenprint and acrylic on panel, 36 × 87 inches, Gift of the artist in honor of Sue Taylor, Ph.D., Portland Art Museum, Portland, Oregon, © Rita Robillard, 2017.96.2.

painted and printed imagery within each piece"; the trees are "pillars and graceful sentries, central to this region's history and beauty."[15] Other works from this series, which combines paintings of trees with etchings of landscapes culled from vintage books in the artist's collection, were completed during a three-month residency at Kala Art Institute in Berkeley and subsequently exhibited in the Kala Artist Residency Exhibition, Augen Gallery, and the Sitka Art Invitational.

In 2017, *Coastal Range* was acquired by the Portland Art Museum. Other works by Robillard are in the collections of the Yale University Art and Architecture Library, the Whitney Museum of American Art Library, the New York Public Library, the MIT Library, and the Los Angeles County Museum of Art. Now housed far from their original home, they convey the artist's particular vision of history and place in the Pacific Northwest.

Foreground (2013–2020)

Robillard was granted emerita status at PSU in 2013, and as her teaching duties lessened, her studio practice and career intensified. In 2014, her work was included in *Women in Print: A Contemporary View* at the Williamson Gallery at Scripps College—an important survey of "outstanding women artists" that placed Robillard's work alongside prints by Sophie Calle, Ellen Gallagher, Julie Mehretu, and Alison Saar, among others. The exhibition essay by curator Margaret Mathews-Berenson cites Robillard as an "artist-explorer, inserting [herself] into an environment and analyzing its past" and notes that there has been a shift in cultural consciousness from the Manifest Destiny heydays of landscape painters such as Albert Bierstadt and Thomas Moran, to a contemporary understanding of the landscape as a site for preservation and caretaking.[16]

The next three bodies of work that Robillard produced deepened her engagement with strategies of layering used to create a sense of moving backward and forward through the physical space depicted in the artwork, as well as along the continuum of the time periods held within the depictions. The twenty-five works in 2014's extensive exhibition *Renewing Time, Caressing the Moment* at Augen Gallery took the landscape as a projection of Portland's aspirations and fantasies by placing an assortment of historical images atop each other to build a dialectic between past and present.

In two different series from this period, *Polarities: Patterns in Time* and *The Waters of March— Spring*, Robillard worked lace patterns into her layers as a way of expressing a sense of domestic caretaking. In these works, she recalls her maternal grandmother's house, where lace doilies protected the household's valuable possessions; she also tapped into her memories of the textiles in the collection of Lacis Museum of Lace and Textiles, a Berkeley archive and

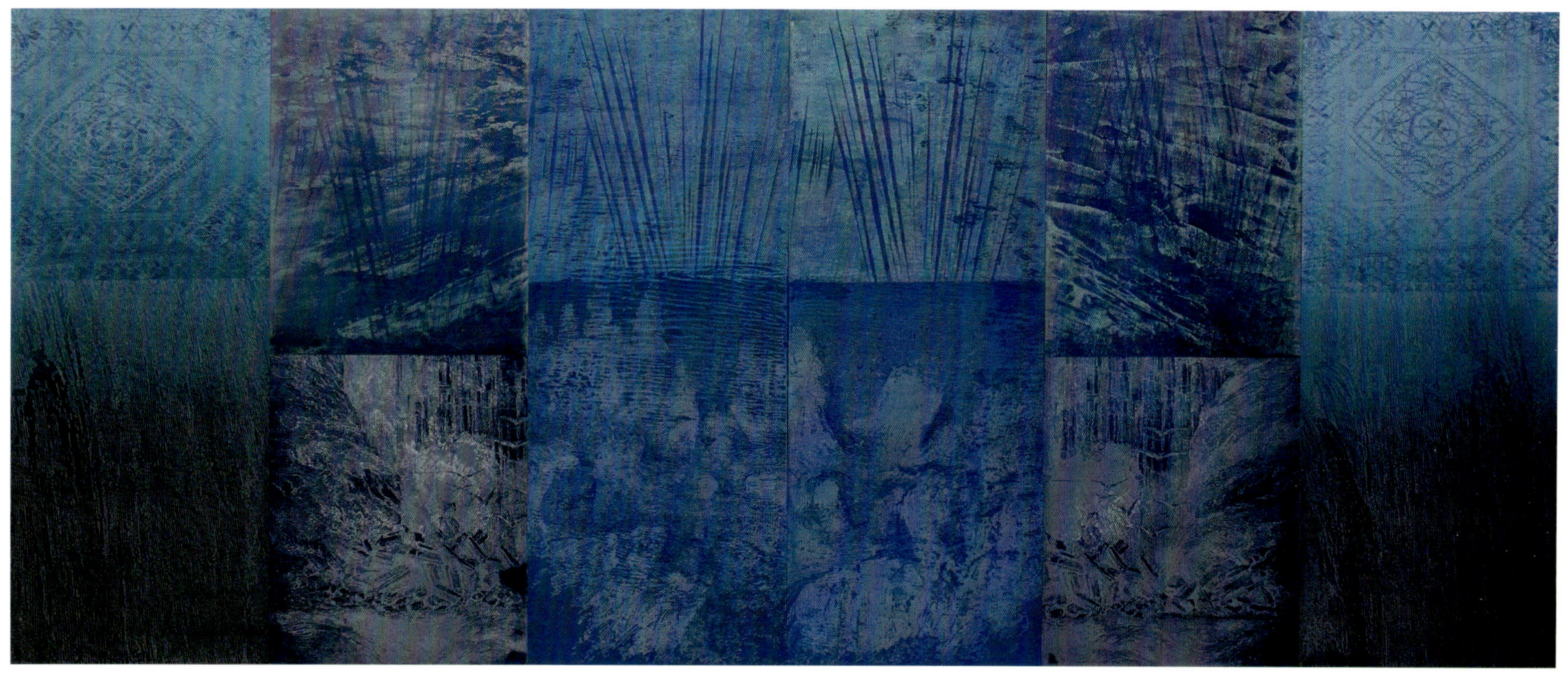

store devoted to the craft of lacemaking, which the artist visited frequently as a student at UC Berkeley. In *Polarities: Patterns in Time*, exhibited in 2016 at Augen Gallery, the artist continued to appropriate images from her thirty-year archive of nineteenth-century books on travel and discovery (fig. 17). In printing these images alongside lace patterns in layers of flat and iridescent colors, sanding, carving, and drawing in between the layers, she simultaneously built toward resolving the final image while variegating the surface in successive strata, much as any forest is shaped by coverings of rain and leaves and contoured by wind and footprints.

Robillard further developed this mode of juxtaposing romantic landscapes with lace in the panels she exhibited in 2019's *The Waters of March—Spring*. In a written statement for the work, she called it "something of an ironic exorcism," using lace as a "wishful shield" to protect a landscape under threat from human activity.[17] In *Orb I* and *Orb II* (figs. 18, 19) the lace pattern is clearly visible, with an abstracted circular floral or web motif rising in the orange background like a sun, easily perceived behind a slope covered with conifers. Yet in the screenprint/paintings of *Falls I*, *Falls II*, and *Falls III* a lace pattern isn't discernible. Instead, the layers of screenprinting—sometimes as many as ten prints, with lines slightly offset and overlapping with one another—give a sense of vibration or optical disturbance that lends a feeling of agitation to the work. Though they contain the same main image of a waterfall cascading down a cliff into a forest stream, the three panels get successively stranger and darker: where *Falls I* (fig. 20) comprises naturalistic tones, *Falls II* (fig. 21) is created in Pop Art shades of turquoise, teal, and orange; while in *Falls III* (fig. 22) the sky behind the falls is a deep twilight blue, and the trees and rocks appear in navy, black, and a golden beige. This twenty-by-twenty-inch panel seems like a long-awaited companion piece to her 1987 painting *Night View* (fig. 5): both evince a quality that could be read as either

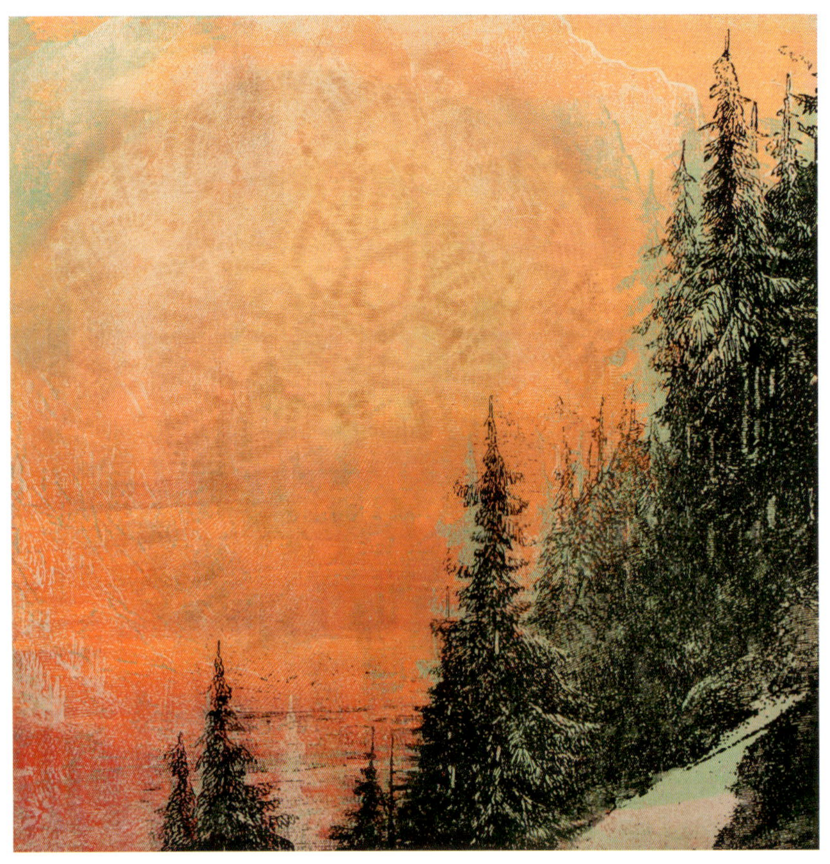

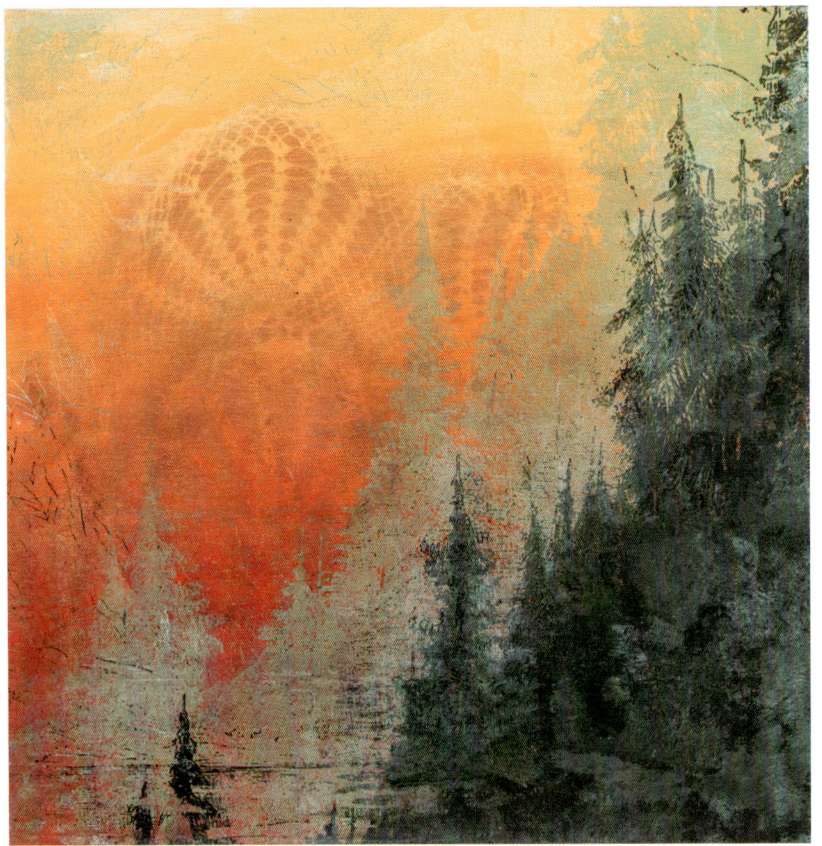

Fig. 18: *Orbs of the Forest I*, from the series *Waters of March—Spring*, 2019, screenprint and acrylic on panel, 18 × 18 inches, courtesy of the artist and Augen Gallery.

Fig. 19: *Orbs of the Forest II*, from the series *Waters of March—Spring*, 2019, screenprint and acrylic on panel, 18 × 18 inches, courtesy of the artist and Augen Gallery.

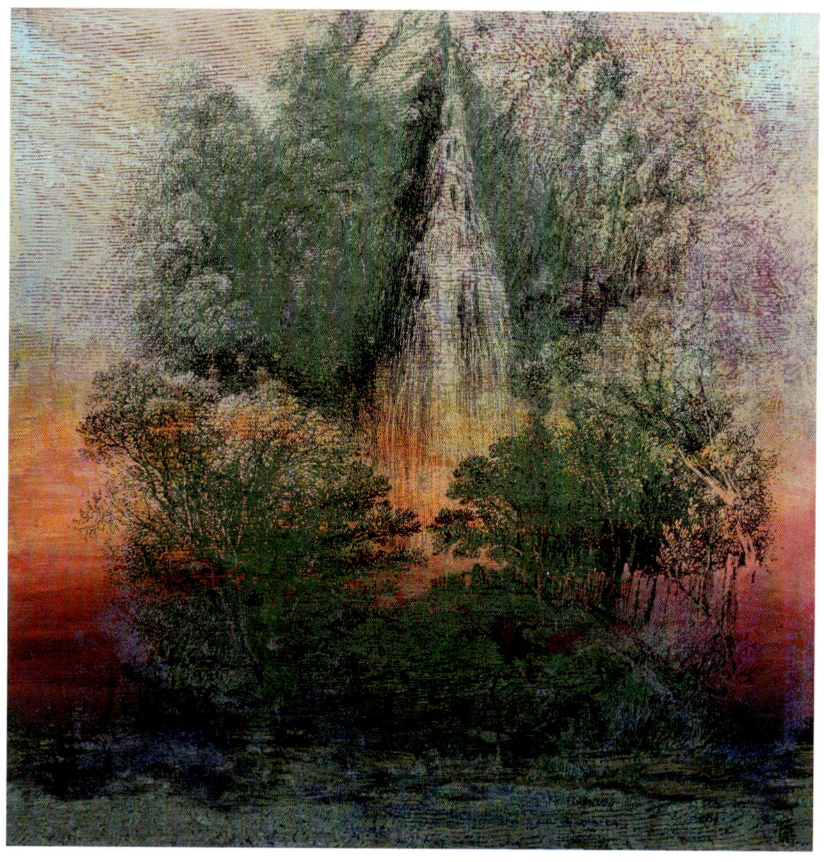

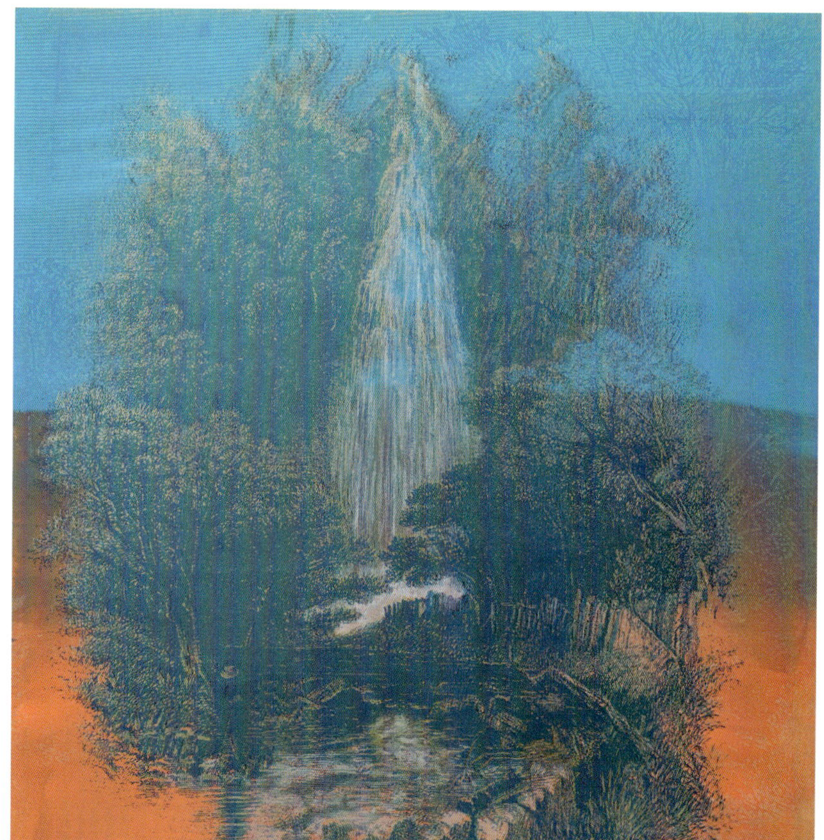

Fig. 20: *Falls I*, from the series *Waters of March—Spring*, 2019, screenprint and acrylic on panel, 20 × 20 inches, courtesy of the artist and the Augen Gallery.

Fig. 21: *Falls II*, from the series *Waters of March—Spring*, 2019, screenprint and acrylic on panel, 20 × 20 inches, courtesy of the artist and the Augen Gallery.

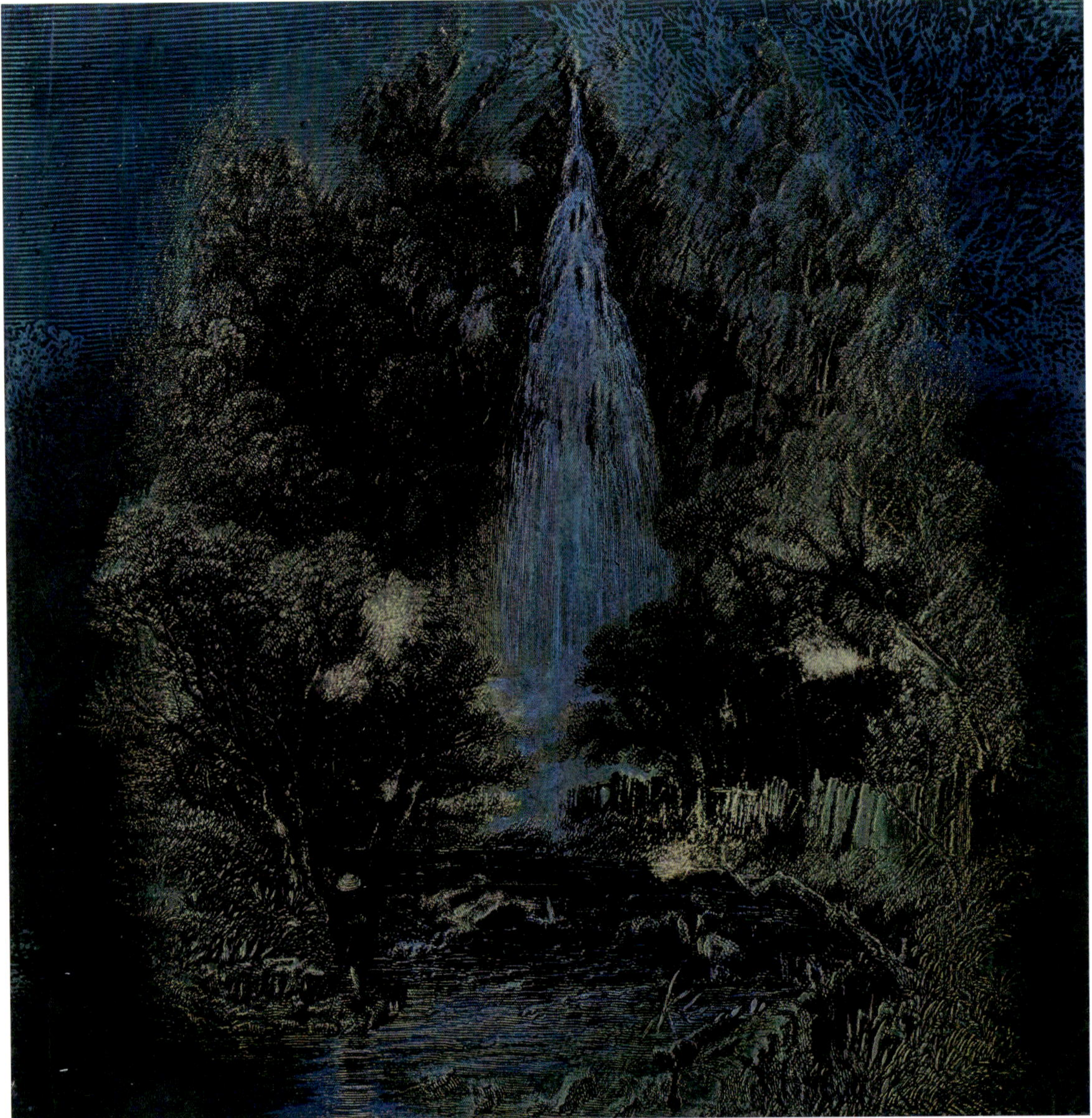

peaceful or ominous. In her studio Robillard told me, "My work puts different ideas together, it takes you to new places. Ultimately, [the viewer's interpretation] is a projection—you see what you want to see."[18]

And how could we not? For many of us, the landscapes that we've come to know represent a simultaneous association of autonomous organic entities, overlaid with cultural and social traditions, crowned by ethics of progress, laws about use, and Eurocentric ideals of human advancement and dominion over the land. I'm reminded of a passage from journalist Timothy Egan's book *The Good Rain*, as he describes the view from the shoreline of the Columbia River near Hanford: "Several generations of history haunt this place. On level ground next to the river is a trio of aging willows, planted for shade by homesteaders who were chased off the land when the bomb builders took over, a rough collision of two eras. Across the river, in the foreground, is a tree with nine blue herons perched on its limbs; in the background is an abandoned nuclear reactor."[19] This kind of historical and experiential haunting is what

Fig. 23: *Spring Poet*, from the series *Flower Serenade: A Gift of Time*, 2020, monoprint with oil pastel on paper, 24 × 17¾ inches, collection of the artist.

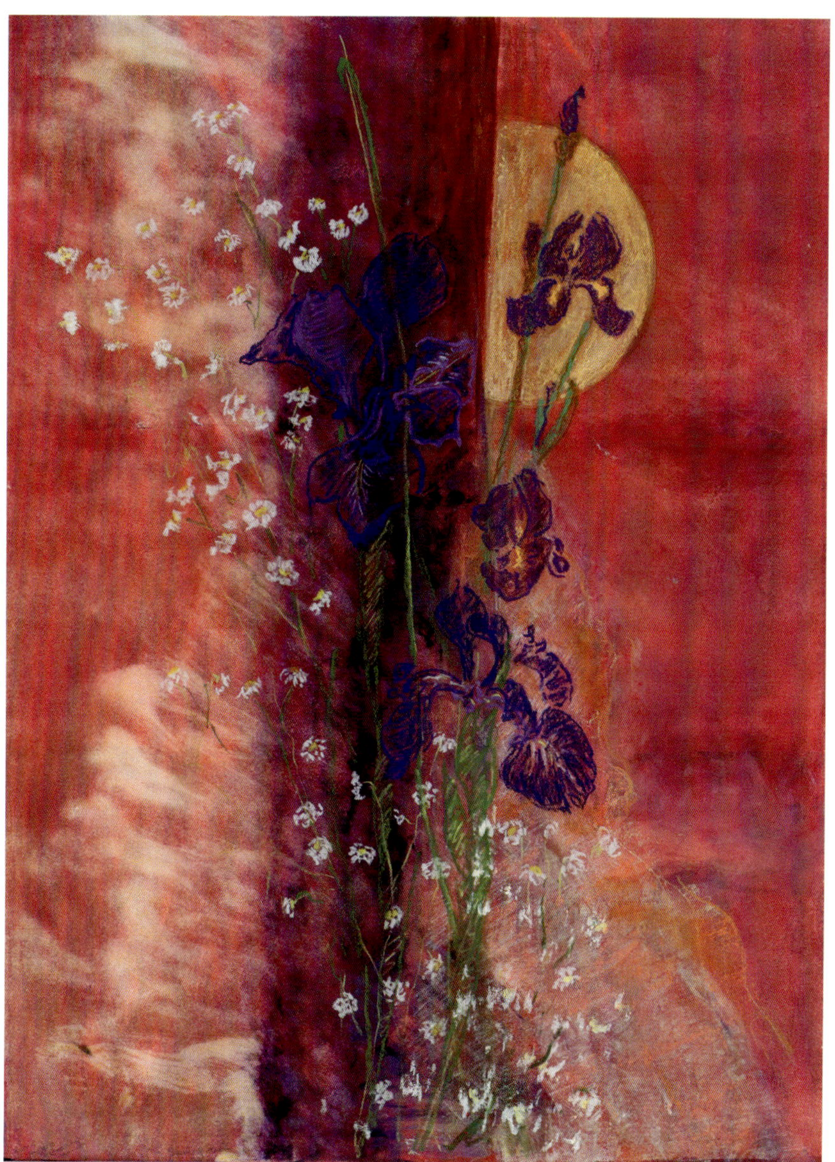

leads viewers to assume that Robillard's work represents a local mountain or forest that they have seen before. In reality, her layered mountains are not actually pictures of Mount Hood, and her *Falls* do not depict the nearby Multnomah Falls, but we associate them all the same because of the way that *landscape* is a nexus point for the eye and the mind's eye, a synchronous meeting point for the physical and psychological attributes of the natural world. We bring what we already know to what we see.

Unity (2020–2022)

Despite the burdens of the pandemic, Robillard continues her active practice. Through the winter and spring of 2020, she exhibited a selection of prints in a mini-retrospective entitled *Votives & Polarities* at the Dengerink Administration Building Gallery at WSU Vancouver. In her studio, she created a suite of new works in screenprint, drawing, and watercolor (fig. 23)

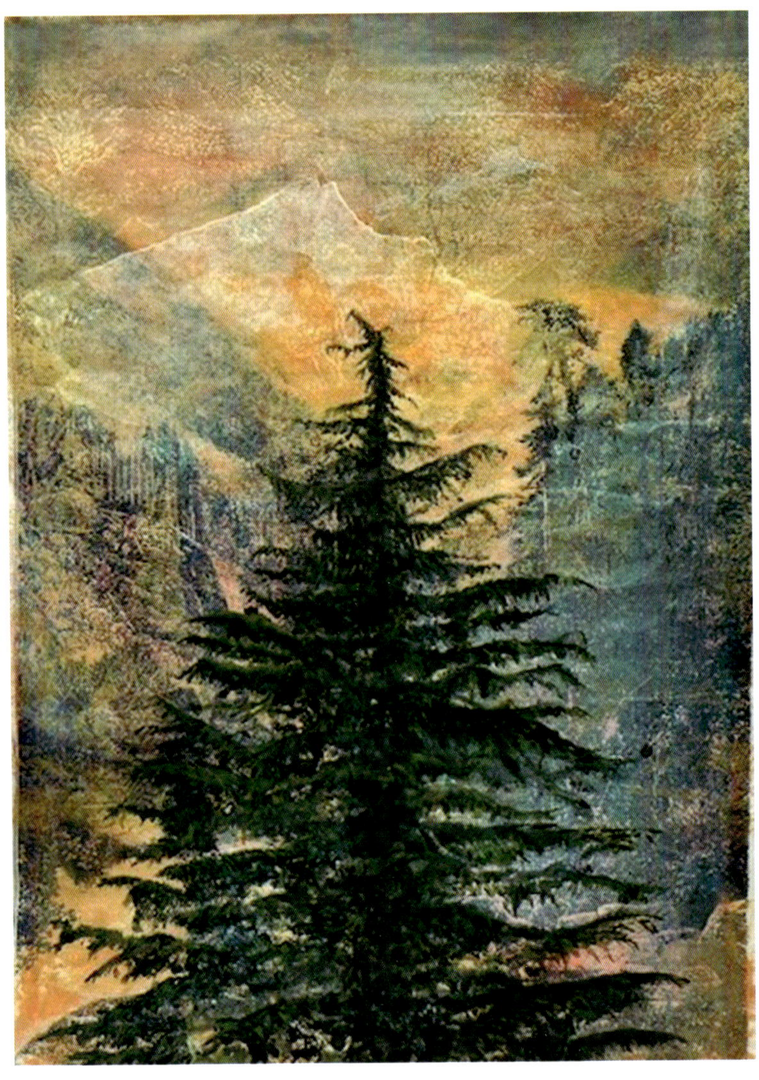

that brought together inspirations from the exhibition *With Pleasure: Pattern and Decoration in American Art 1972–1985* (which she saw at MOCA Los Angeles in early 2020) with her reactions to the deprivations of self-isolation: Some of these works, such as *Grace*, *Double Delight*, and *A Family Affair* depict formal and casual arrangements of flowers in vases—a common source of solace in lockdown. Larger works such as *Solo Dancer I* (fig. 24), *Dusk* (fig. 25), and *Nesting* (fig. 1) show solitary trees—hemlocks—rising in front of distant vistas shrouded in yellow haze. These works culminated in her 2021 exhibition *Flower Serenade: A Gift of Time* at Augen Gallery. That same year, Robillard's prints were included in "Visions of Eternity," an online concert of music by composer Andrea Reinkemeyer, performed by the vocal ensemble In Mulieribus. Additionally, she gave a virtual talk on her work to the community of ecoartspace.org, a platform for artists addressing environmental issues, and attended the McCanna House Artist-in-Residence Program at the North Dakota Museum of Art.

In one of our conversations about her practice, the artist said, "I don't really believe art is going to change things," while in another, she said, "Art is not a political vehicle; it doesn't give us a solution to the problems."[20] She didn't offer either of these statements with rancor—

Fig. 24: *Solo Dancer I*, from the series *Flower Serenade: A Gift of Time*, 2020, hand-colored digital print on gampi paper, 22 × 16 inches, courtesy of the artist and the Augen Gallery.

she meant them pragmatically, as a way of sorting art from activism. Her meaning is clear in the contrast between art's oblique approach and the efficacy of direct actions like marches, protests, tree sitting, lobbying, and other campaigns. Yet art can proffer a perspective that stimulates the expression of environmental ethics. Artistic landscapes have always been an expression of values and a form of cultural geography, helping to communicate the dynamics of landscape change, projecting the meanings and importance of place. In our current age, a painting of a tree does not supply an immediate answer to the climate crisis, but it conveys the investment of the artist and the ethos of the society in which it's created. In an exhibition of these works, the affective state of the viewer becomes the point, with its attendant potential to shape the future.

Wes Jackson, founder of the Land Institute in Salina, Kansas, has said: "It has never been our national goal to become native to this place. It has never seemed necessary even to begin such a journey. And now, almost too late, we perceive its necessity."[21] I return to looking at Robillard's *Nesting*, the lone tree that's silhouetted against a misty vista of distant valley and mountain. This view is of a type that is achievable only at the end of a long trek through time and space. Thus it not only reveals the beauty of the natural landforms but illuminates the way in which we see the world within the contexts of our histories, our desires, our fears, and even the sense-memories that accompany the act of looking. *Nesting* evokes the soft crush of pine needles underfoot, the damp resinous odor of the trees, the fresh chill of the mist, and the feeling, above all, of being both alone in the wilderness and not alone, of looking at the landscape and—for a moment—knowing that we are part of it.

Bean Gilsdorf is an artist and writer. Her work has been exhibited at the Museum of Contemporary Art Santa Barbara, the Wattis Institute, and the American Textile History Museum, among others. She is the recipient of numerous awards, including an Andy Warhol Foundation Arts Writers Grant, two creative Fulbright Fellowships to Poland, and a Graduate Fellowship at Headlands Center for the Arts.

Notes

1   Rita Robillard, artist statement from www.RitaRobillard.com.

2   Rita Robillard, exhibition statement from MFA Thesis Exhibition, 1981. From the artist's own ephemera.

3   Interview with the artist, February 13, 2022.

4   Barry Lopez, "The American Geographies," in *About This Life: Journeys on the Threshold of Memory* (New York: Knopf, 1998).

5   Interview with the artist, February 13, 2022.

6   Helen Slade, "Yes, in My Back Yard?: An Exhibition Time Line Living Documentary Resource Library" (exhibition brochure) (Richland, WA: Allied Arts Gallery, 1993).

7   Rita Robillard, untitled statement for the series *Votives for Hanford*, 2020. From the artist's own ephemera.

8   Interview with the artist, February 13, 2022.

9   Yi-Fu Tuan, "Thought and Landscape: The Eye and the Mind's Eye," in *The Interpretation of Ordinary Landscapes*, ed. D. W. Meinig (Oxford: Oxford University Press, 1979).

10 Sue Taylor, "Rita Robillard at Elizabeth Leach," *Art in America*, May 2002.

11 Taylor, "Rita Robillard at Elizabeth Leach."

12 Interview with the artist, April 21, 2022.

13 Aldo Leopold, *A Sand County Almanac* (New York: Oxford University Press, 1949). See also https://www.aldoleopold.org/about/the-land-ethic/.

14 Sue Taylor, "Rita Robillard's 'Poetical Cosmology,'" in *Place in Time: Contemporary Landscape* (exhibition catalog) (Claremont, CA: Scripps College, 2008).

15 Rita Robillard, artist statement for "And Then Again . . ." from www.RitaRobillard.com.

16 Margaret Mathews-Berenson, *Women in Print: A Contemporary View* (exhibition catalog) (Claremont, CA: Williamson Gallery at Scripps College, 2014).

17 Rita Robillard, artist statement for "The Waters of March–Spring" from www.RitaRobillard.com.

18 Interview with the artist, April 21, 2022.

19 Timothy Egan, *The Good Rain: Across Time and Terrain in the Pacific Northwest* (New York: Knopf, 1990).

20 Interviews with the artist, February 13, 2022, and April 21, 2002.

21 Wes Jackson, *Becoming Native to This Place* (Lexington: University Press of Kentucky, 1994).

Fig. 25: *Dusk*, from the series *Flower Serenade: A Gift of Time*, 2020, screenprint and pencil on paper, 26½ × 17½ inches, courtesy of the artist and the Augen Gallery.

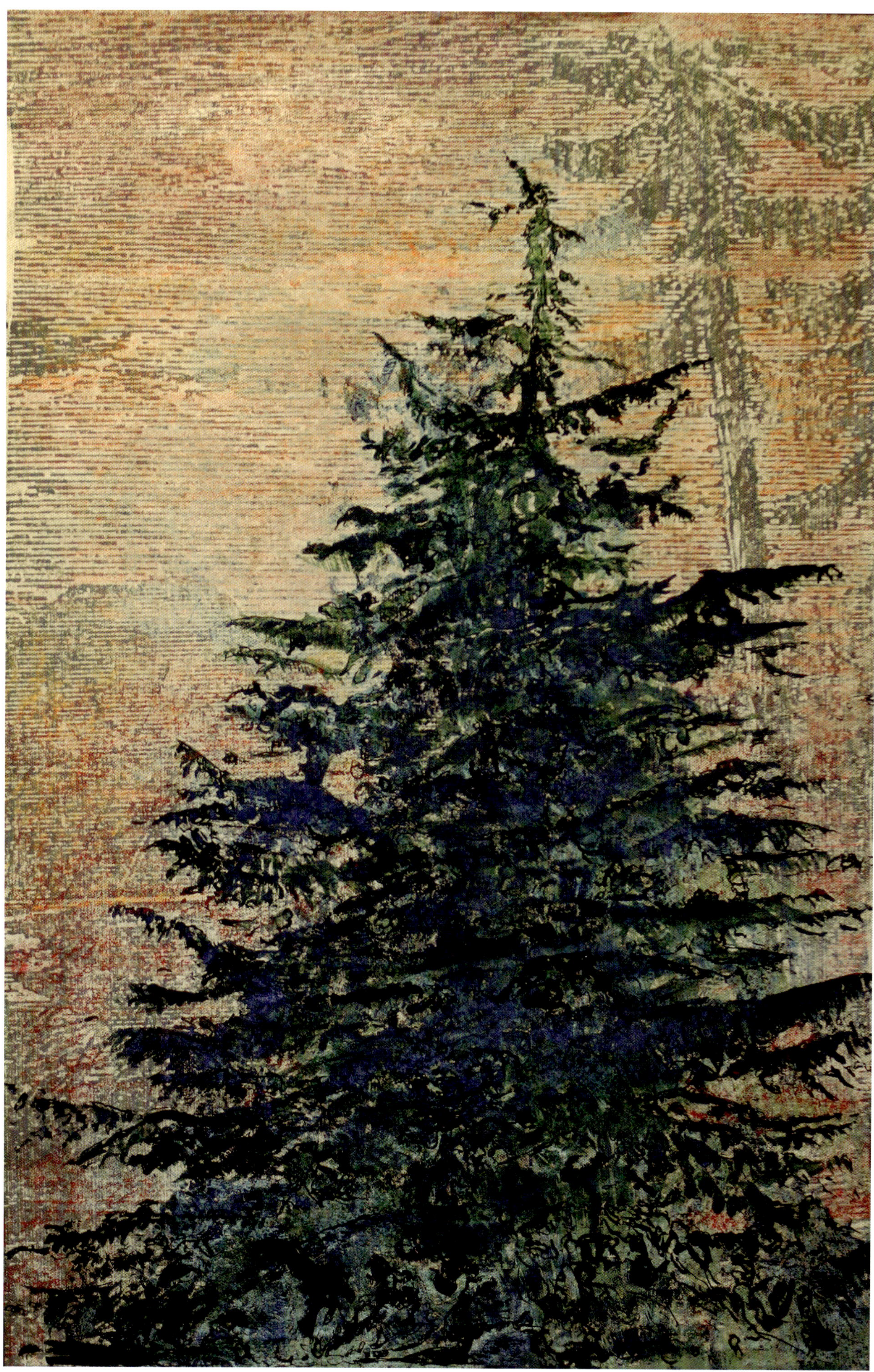

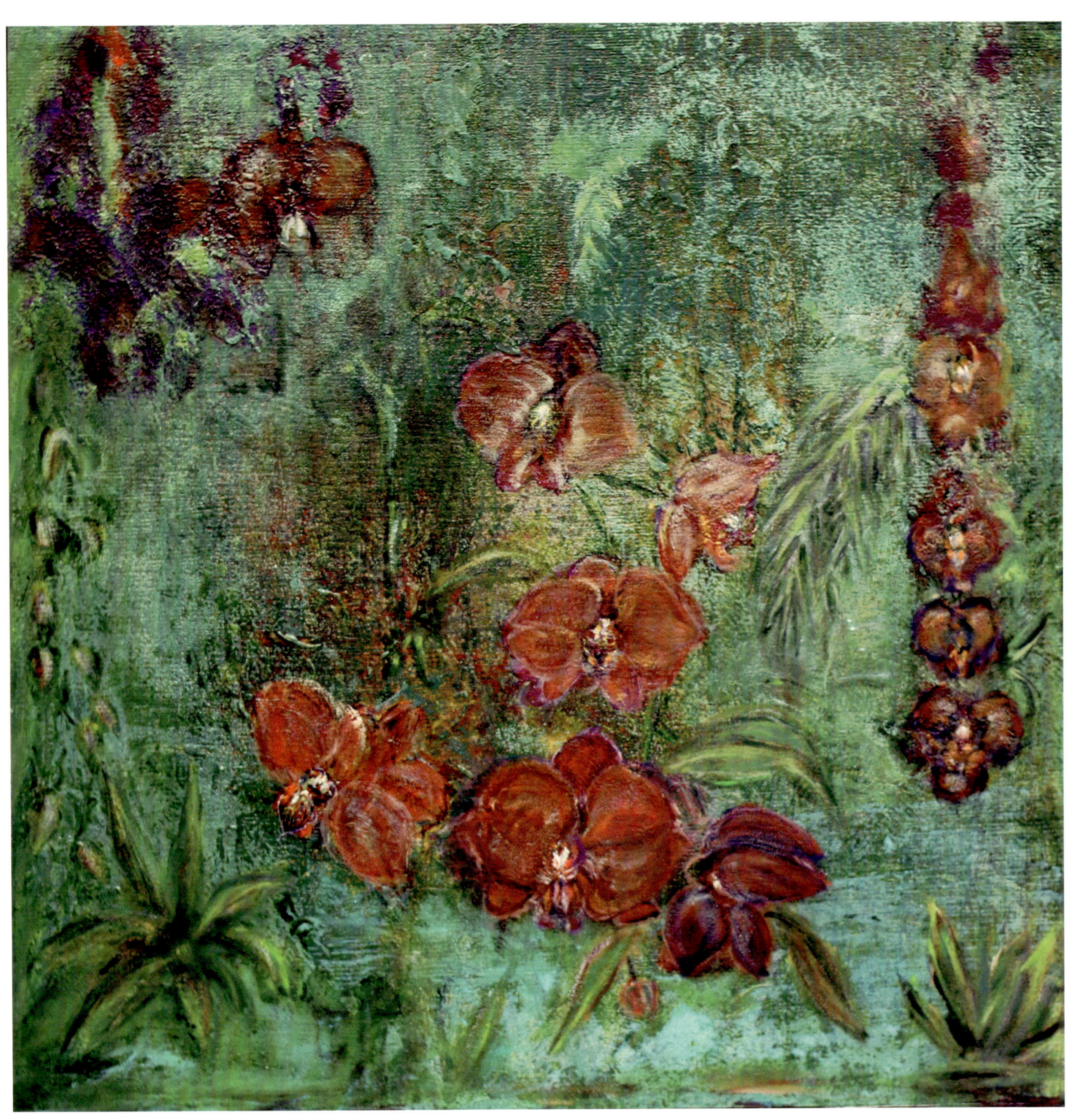

Talking with Rita Robillard

Frances DeVuono

This interview is a composite of conversations Rita Robillard and I had during April and May 2020.

FDeV: *I think there is a hunger to better know mid- and late-twentieth-century women artists right now. I say that because the last decade has brought forth a plethora of undervalued and undershown women's work from that period. I am thinking of Maria Lassnig's Golden Lion award at the 2013 Venice Biennale, which she received when she was ninety-one, Senga Nengudi's major international exhibitions during 2014 and 2018, Luchita Hurtado's recent show at LACMA at age one hundred, the posthumous rediscovery of Hilma af Klimt's work, and so many more. It's as if we need to know that part of our collective history. So in that light, I want to ask you a few questions about how you got to where you are as an artist. I know you were born in New York City.*

RR: Yes, my parents moved there from the Midwest. My father was a musician who had a band and worked in early television and on Broadway. So I got to see plays and musicals and went to museums very early in my life. The Met [Metropolitan Museum of Art] was free then, so whenever things got difficult in my family—and they did—those kinds of things were my escape. New York is both a great and a difficult place for a young girl to grow up in. You know, I grew up under the climate of McCarthyism on the New York music and entertainment world. As a kid when answering the phone, I remember actually being told to divulge no information, to say "I know nothing" if anyone asked questions. Seeing that kind of adult fear as a child is memorable.

By the time I was ten, I took public transportation all over the city, and its cultural aspects kept me going. New York was rich in so many ways—not just museums. I remember going to the apartment of this Swedish friend, Astrid, who lived in Spanish Harlem. It was a six-flight walk-up, and she had this Puerto Rican neighbor whose family would invite us in and teach us how to do the merengue and salsa. I couldn't have been more than thirteen years old.

Brazilian Dreams, from the series *Polarities: Patterns in Time: 1880/2016, 2.3 Degrees Fahrenheit*, 2018, screenprint and oil on panel, 20 × 20 inches, courtesy of the artist and Augen Gallery.

My family didn't have money—we lived in a rent-controlled building—but there was a lot of free cultural stuff, like the early Happenings. I remember seeing John Cage once at a Monday-night lecture at Cooper Union when I was still in high school. Even though home life was tough after my father died when I was twelve and I have a younger sister who has severe but not understood disabilities that made my mother's life very challenging, the city was my solace.

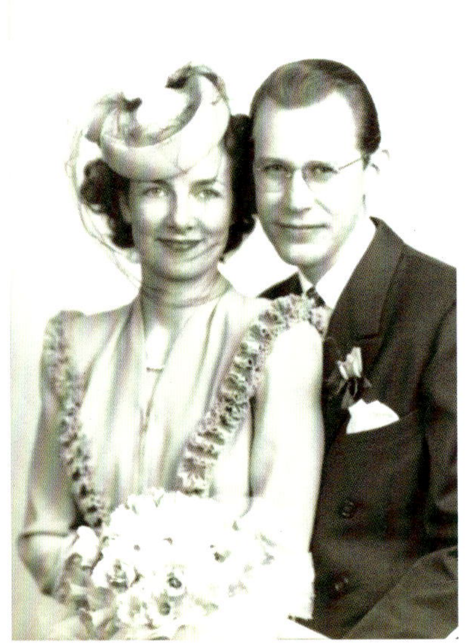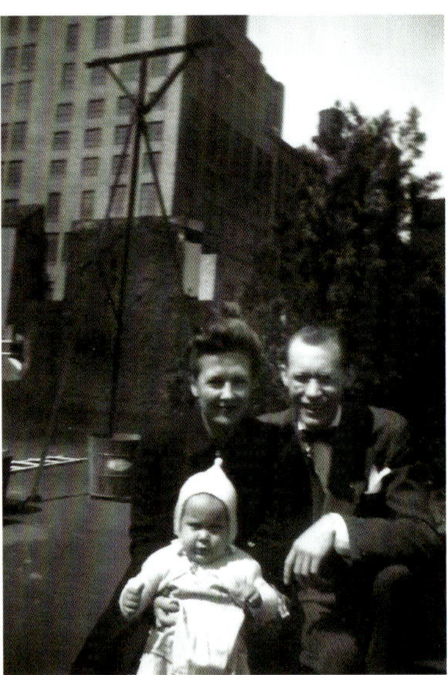

FDeV: *You went to Cooper Union—that was the aspirational school for artists when I was young as, until a few years ago, it was free for anyone who got in. What inspired you to apply?*

RR: Hmm . . . I was lucky to go to terrific public city schools. I went to Washington Irving High School. It was all girls with exceptional teachers, especially in art. We had four periods of art a day. One of my teachers there, Sarah Slotkin, encouraged me to take the test for Cooper Union. Since it was basically free and was the only way I could attend college, I applied. It was funny. I remember getting the acceptance letter from Cooper Union and I was so happy, but you know when you are a first-generation [college] student, you just don't understand how things work. So, while I was delighted, I didn't know I was supposed to reply back until another letter from them arrived assuming I'd declined. It began by saying, "We're so sorry . . ." I called them immediately and it got all straightened out in the end.

I'd met my husband at the original Cedar Bar when I was sixteen, and we married right after I finished high school. In addition to being married, I was also working, so I attended Cooper Union at night.

The school was very formal at that time—very Bauhaus-oriented in terms of design. It was really classical and I had only male art teachers, some of whom were really great. I took a class in materials with Charlie Seide, who was a prominent advocate for bringing back methods of varnishes and encaustic. But the climate was different. For example, we were invited to talk after classes over a beer. That would be a tremendous time for mentoring, a casual atmosphere where the lines between faculty and students could be loosened. The problem was that the chosen bar was a place called McSorley's. And this was in the late '60s and McSorley's didn't admit women!

FDeV: *Then you moved to California. You showed me a photo of a diptych,* The Hero and the Hero's Sweetheart, *that you did during that time. It's unlike others I have seen in that it is so sharp and graphic.*

RR: Yes, we did move to California, first to LA in 1968. Then we moved to San Francisco right after my second daughter was born, and we lived there for three years. *The Hero and the Hero's Sweetheart?* I only have photos of it now, but in retrospect, I think it was an early moment for me—and others—about women's roles, questions about identity. . . . The paintings are huge and I gave them to friends before we left for Brazil.

FDcV: *How do you think the time in Brazil affected your work?*

RR: We wanted to live and work someplace outside the USA. The Peace Corps was big at that time, but with two children that wasn't a possibility for us. So we ended up in Brazil, living in São Paulo for two and a half years and then spending the last six months in a rural area. I taught art in a kind of Head Start program and, through the kids, learned so much about Brazilian culture. The tropics—with all its flora and fauna—was incredibly intoxicating. I had a studio and participated in a few exhibitions with Brazilian artists. Just being there gave me the time and opportunity to do things I'd never done before—from watching a butterfly come out of a chrysalis to going to religious ceremonies, ones that had originally come to Brazil with the African diaspora during the slave trade. That dance and music have influenced me ever since.

Before we went, I'd taken a Latin American history class at City College and learned something about Brazilian history, but I was surprised by how welcomed I was at some of the Candomblé (Macumba is another name for it) ceremonies. I loved the syncopated rhythms. They were familiar in a way, bringing back fond memories of how I used to make my father play boogie-woogie over and over again on the piano as a child.

I'd known about Greek and Western mythology, of course, but learning about the Candomblé was revelatory—because music is so dominant. Their drumming is sacred. I continued studying parts of these religions when I returned to the USA. At Berkeley, much to my delight, I discovered that Cal's Doe Library had a huge collection of the Candomblé liturgies, and I composed a bibliography of these works. It was long ago, but the experiences in Brazil were a big influence on who I am as an artist and a person.

FDcV: *When you returned to the US in 1974, you entered UC Berkeley, where you received your MFA. Can you talk about that time?*

RR: I think that having been a wife and mother so young, my time at UC Berkeley was important. It allowed me to develop, to grow in so many ways. Let me think, there was so much . . .

When I got to the MFA program at Cal, I decided to focus on printmaking. I already had my own painting studio by then and wanted to learn something at Cal that used their facilities—

something that I couldn't get on my own. By the time I was in grad school, Sylvia Lark was a new member of the faculty, and her specialty was photoetching and other photo processes. So as a student I learned those, and ended up running the art department's photo print studio in a work-study position. I was also doing installations at the time, but my early work was photo-based. Even with the installations, I was documenting them and incorporating that documentation into prints and mixed-media work.

I had two children at the time and was recently divorced, so my studio schedule was once again in the evenings—from twelve o'clock at night until six in the morning. It was crazy, but fun. I think it helped that I was older and had lots of life experience. I became friends with the janitors, who would bring me cookies, and, as engrossed in the work as I might be, I knew that when the man with keys came at 6:00 a.m., it was time for me to leave.

One of the first things I did as a student at Cal was a "manifesto" that compared an impossibly small, size 4.5 mannequin's foot in a six-inch high heel with my own ample footprint of 8.5. It was as if I could suddenly laugh at all those 1950s conventions of what it meant to be female in a new light, losing the white gloves and girdles. It was a liberation.

Another early project was a video of a man and a woman walking nude through the art building. Looking back, I think it was an attempt to critique the institution, to highlight our vulnerability within that place. That is how I saw it then; I felt very lucky to be there. I was using a Sony Portapak, so the end result was rough, but none of this was done for posterity. It was really playful. We were exploring ourselves and what art we could make.

There was so much at Cal. I had another great teacher, Frances Butler, who taught design and typography. We learned to print broadsides on an actual Gutenberg press that was in the basement of the Bancroft Library.

And then I did an installation called *One Point Perspective*, focusing on all the doors to Kroeber Hall. I used electrical tape. This was '79–'80. It was odd, because when you were in the building looking outside, the space was really open, but from the outside looking in, the building became tunnelled. I thought it made a likely metaphor for academic research— the need to get narrower and more specific. Using that installation as a basis, I created this series of mixed-media prints that had doors made of balsa wood and mulberry paper attached. When you opened the doors up, there were these very fluid etchings inside, which later became the basis for my thesis work, called *Spirit Ground*. In retrospect, I see these installations, and that early work, as my examination of place: where I was as a graduate student, as an artist, as a mother, all of that—as well as the institution itself.

FDeV: *Do you think* Spirit Ground *was also reflective of your time in Brazil?*

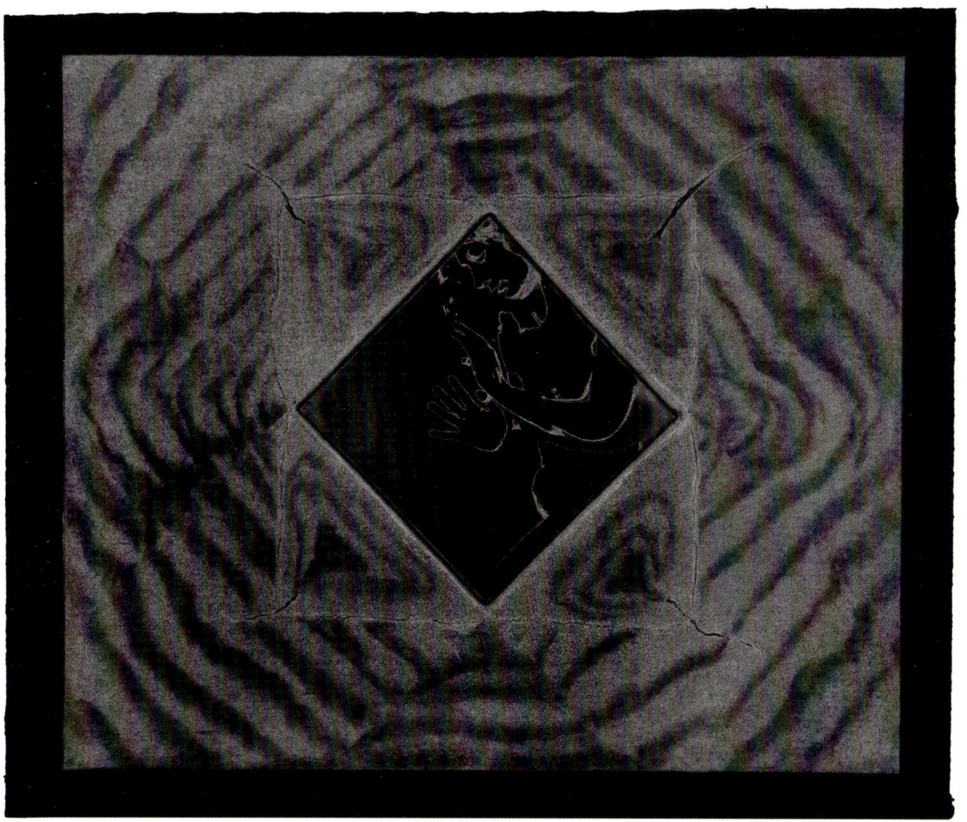

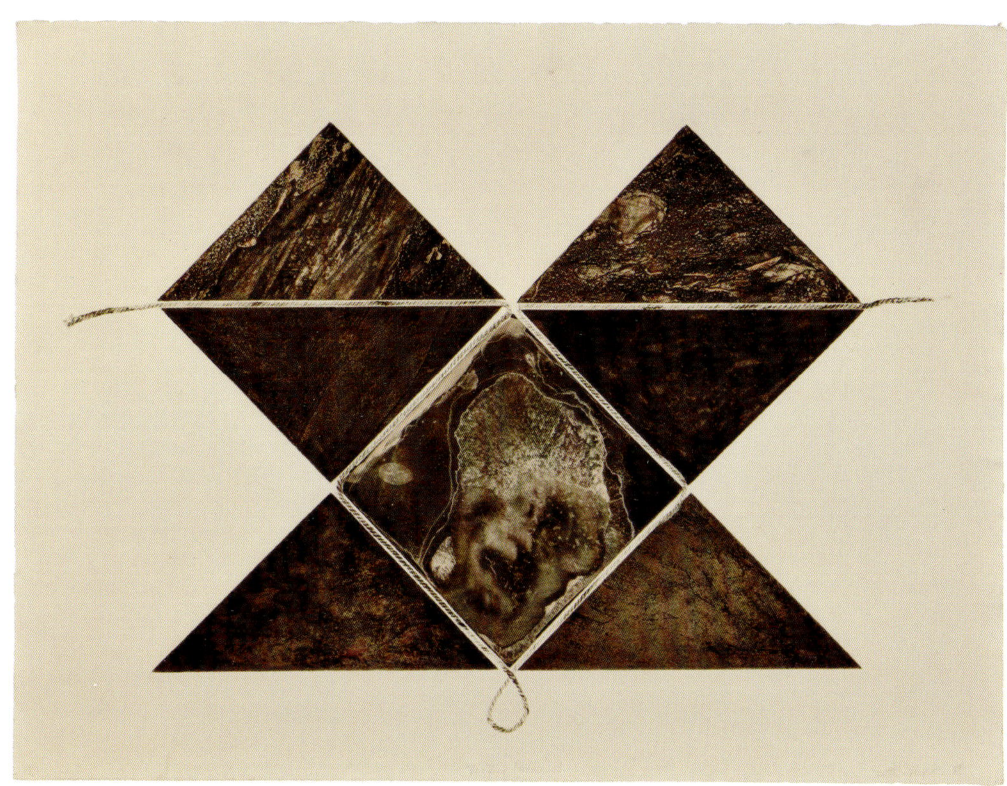

Fig. 26: *Holding Patterns*, from the series *Spirit Ground*, 1978, etching on black paper, 22 × 26¾ inches, courtesy of the artist and the Augen Gallery.

Fig. 27: *Holding Patterns: Pull*, from the series *Spirit Ground*, 1979, etching on gray paper, 22 × 29¾ inches, courtesy of the artist and the Augen Gallery.

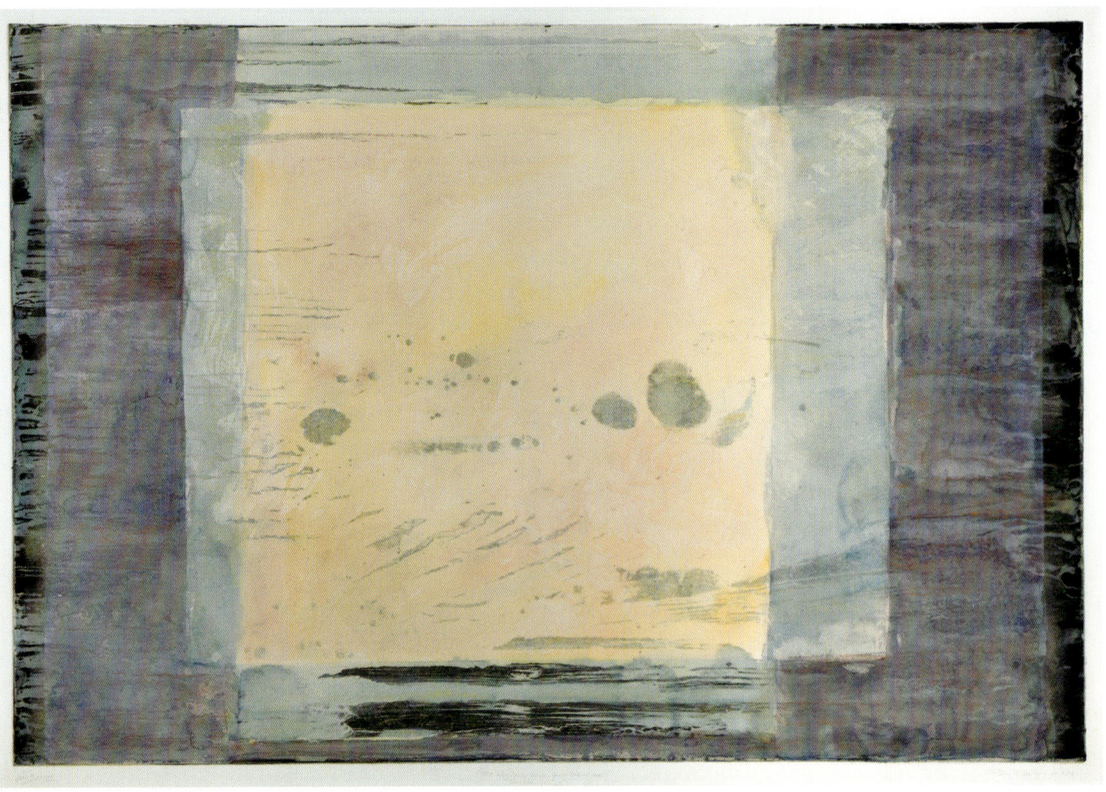

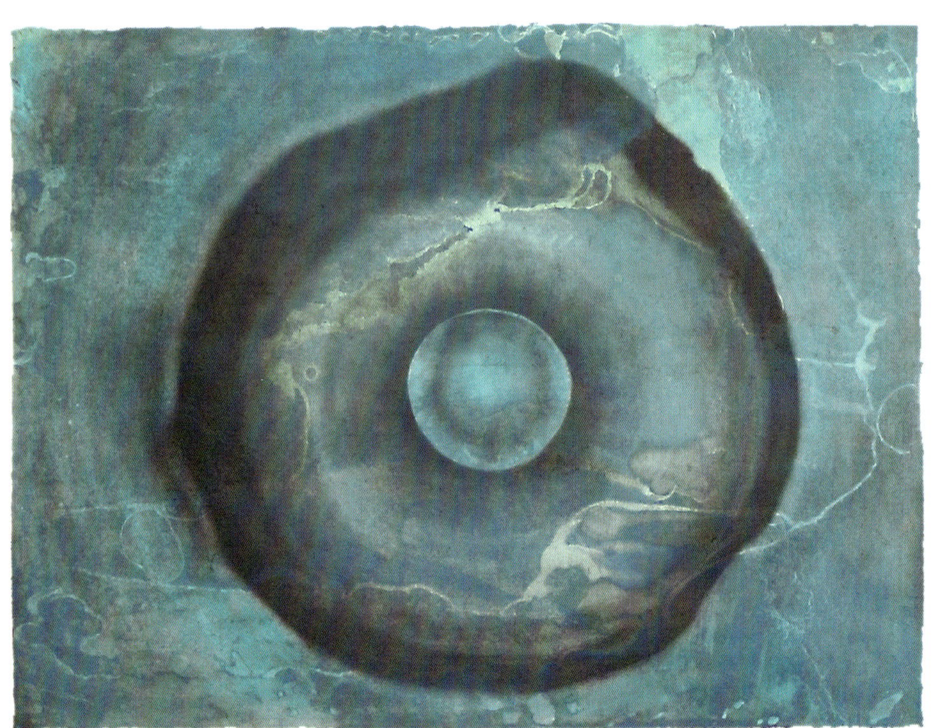

Fig. 28: *Harold's View*, from the series *Spirit Ground*, 1980, etching on paper, 24 × 35½ inches, collection of the artist.

Fig. 29: *Baptismal Whorl*, from the series *Spirit Ground*, 1980, intaglio on paper, 22 × 30 inches, collection of Deborah and Martin Merkle.

RR: Clearly, the *Spirit Ground* work (figs. 26, 27, 28) was influenced by having been in Brazil. There is a river in Minas Gerais called Sumidouro, which means to go underground—to vanish, to disappear. The whole area is rich with petroglyphs, caves with stalactites and stalagmites; it's just a very mystical place, and I think that influenced my thesis work a great deal. Those prints were intaglio (fig. 29), and I used a kind of viscosity printing and a process that Stanley Hayter had developed with a liquid aquatint so you could paint it right on the surface. I was using this reticulating tusche process on top of the aquatint with plates that then were twenty-four by thirty-six inches. The rollers were huge, and to do the process I had to take over the entire printmaking studio—another reason to work at night.

At the time Elmer Bischoff called me a "visionary artist." I wasn't quite sure what that meant. I think maybe he meant Morris Graves—but also the other Northwest artists, and I have to say I do relate to all of them. They were so obvious about being influenced by Asian art. Although I took several anthropology classes, Asian art courses were the only art history classes I took while at Cal. Coming from New York, I wasn't that impressed by many of the collections and shows in the Bay Area museums until I found what was then called the Brundage Collection, which is now, of course, the Asian Art Museum.

FDeV: *You've talked about Sylvia Lark. In what specific ways did she influence you?*

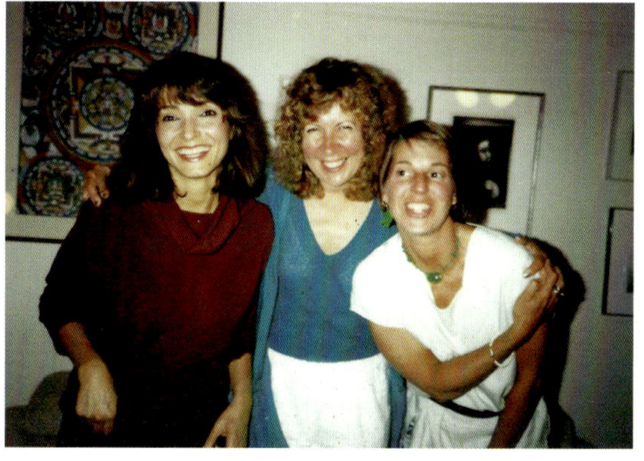

Left to right, Sylvia Lark, Rita Robillard, and Nancy Macko, at Sylvia's house, Berkeley, California, 1985.

RR: Starting off: Sylvia was the first woman I had as an art teacher outside of high school or grade school, you know, as an art professor. She taught me how to write grants. She encouraged me to join organizations such as the California Society of Printmakers, because belonging to these organizations was a way of exhibiting your work. I appreciated her advice and eventually joined their board. She also encouraged me to join the Women's Caucus for Art, and I was on the board of that as well. She really taught all of us how to become professional artists, something most faculty at that time didn't want to talk about. And something I certainly hadn't gotten as an undergraduate. For women especially, it was important to know how to do these things. There were all these steps she taught us—and not just me: there was a whole group of us, and we're all still friends.

FDeV: *And after graduating you worked at the San Francisco Art Institute and UC Davis . . .*

RR: I also taught at Kala Art Institute. After we got a grant for a new process camera at Cal, the old one was given to Kala, and I went there and taught photo processes. But I should mention that in addition to the teaching, I was also able to work at a commercial printshop

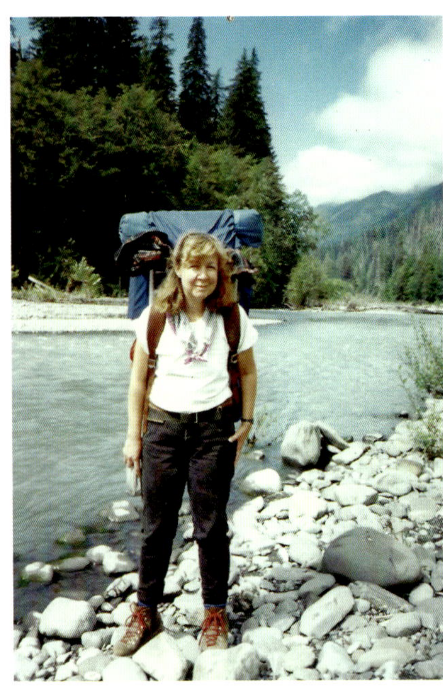

using the skills Sylvia taught me. I worked there 6:00 a.m. to 4:00 p.m., three days a week, to support my adjunct teaching positions. I was also exploring the technology of the time in my own work as well. I joined a group called YLEM [Artists Using Science and Technology] and got a residency at Via Video, where I learned how to create and edit videos, which I also took to later art practice and teaching jobs.

FDeV: *You kept links with California, and you often describe it as having a big impact on your work.*

RR: It did, it did. For many summers when I lived there, I went hiking and backpacking in the Sierras. And who knew I could carry a thirty-five- or forty-pound pack for a week? I went with a friend that I met at Cal, Emily. Her father was a famous Sierra Club leader, so, at first we went with him, and then we went on our own. Of course, I was enthralled—by both the beauty and the difficulty. It was during those early hikes that fire became a visual symbol for my work. I remember one time we came down a ridge and saw a bunch of smoke in front of us. It was terrifying as we really didn't know if we had to go through it to get down to the other side or not. So, fires in the wilderness really caught my imagination and I've done whole series of work about fires over the years: *Vesta Swamp, Conflagrations and Rain* (fig. 30), *Lookout/Outlook* (fig. 8)….You know, if you're not Turner, fire is an incredibly difficult thing to paint.

FDeV: *You've mentioned that salsa dancing or social dancing is a big part of your life.*

Well, I do both. I love Latin dancing. I have always tried to squeeze that into my life. I think it is the opposite of my art making in that it's freeing. The rhythm just takes you, rather than being so layered and detailed. It takes me out of my head. The other thing is that while art making is often a solitary activity, social dancing gets me out.

FDeV: *I first heard of you when you co-chaired the College Art Association's national conference in Seattle, and you seemed like such an activist at the time; do you consider activism an important part of your work?*

RR: I do consider activism an important part of my life. I am not so sure that it is exactly an important part of my artwork in that I don't think art functions in that way. In terms of activism, it started early. Remember, I am of an age where we had duck-and-cover drills in grade school, so by high school I was a member of SANE [National Committee for a Sane

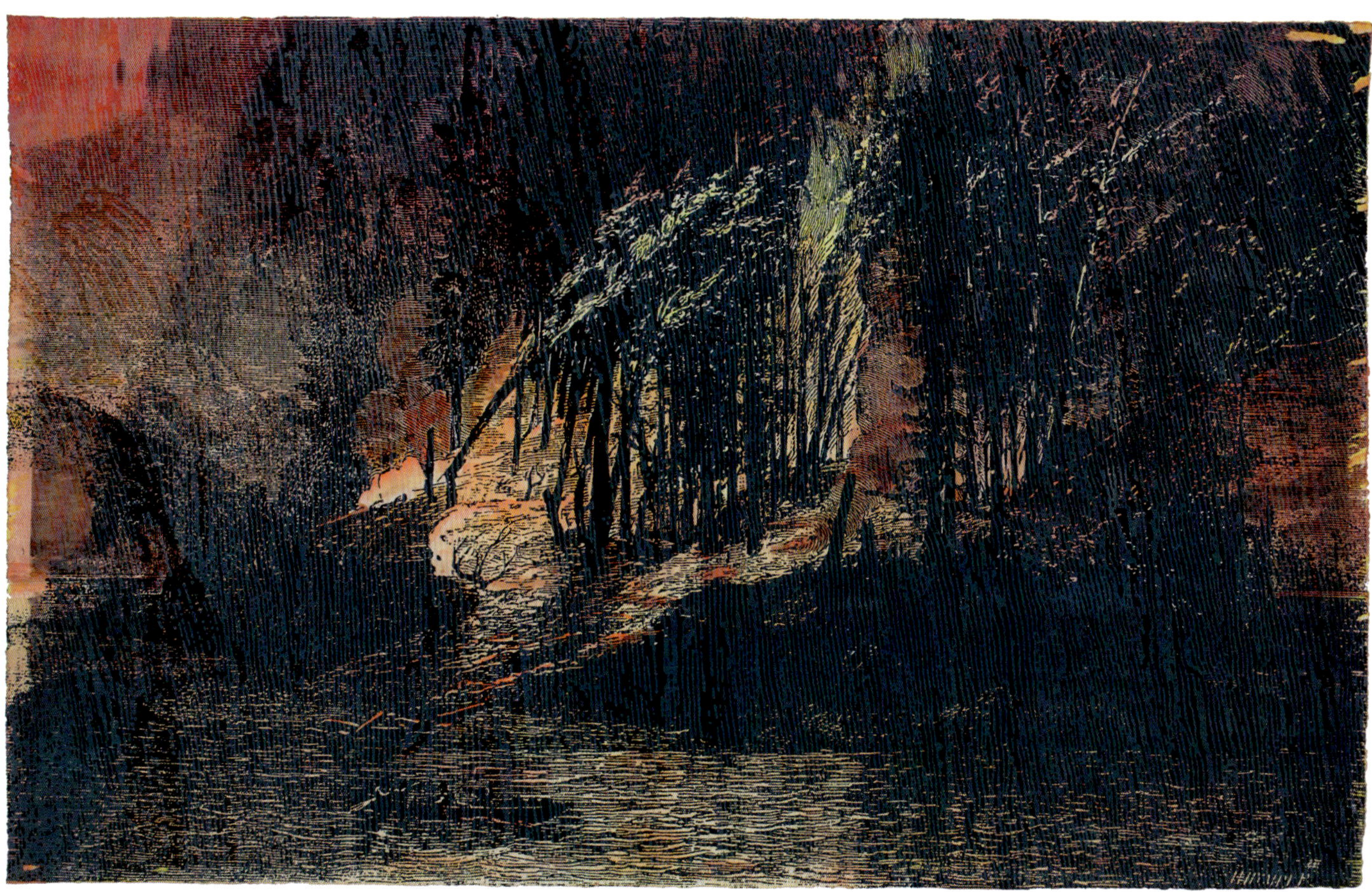

Fig. 30: *Conflagrations and Rain*, from the series *Polarities: Patterns in Time: 1880/2016, 2.3 Degrees Fahrenheit*, 2016, screenprint on paper, 22 × 36 inches, courtesy of the artist and the Augen Gallery.

Nuclear Policy]. And there was the war in Vietnam, civil rights, and feminism. It was the times, but it was also a series of things that I was very passionate about.

In Seattle, Norie Sato and I titled the conference "Artist as World Citizen." For one, we wanted to create a conference that would be more inclusive of practicing artists rather than people just reading papers, so we planned workshops and performances, but we also wanted to be more inclusive of artists. We really wanted a greater diversity of all kinds of people. It was after that conference that I was invited to join the board of the CAA as well as the board of *Art Journal* [one of the two official journals of the CAA].

FDeV: *Retrospectives are an opportunity to make connective threads, and I think viewers will do that in seeing your work. Interest in ecologies, specific historical interventions with nature, the role of women—I see that all as layered in the processes you use in your prints. But if you had to sum up a dominant concept that you've wrestled with throughout your work as an artist, what would it be?*

RR: Well, it is important to me to create a sensual, a kind of tactile, visual language. Traditional etching is generally known for its use of line, yet what interests me are surface qualities. I've always worked with that, early on in etching and up to my current work in screenprinting. I also use those textures—those surfaces—as ways to show histories. But if I have to choose a dominant concept, I think it is place that has always concerned me.

I think every place I've lived has changed my work in some way, and I am also interested in how others perceive the places they are in. For example, shortly after arriving in Portland, I had thirteen people take me to the place that they considered to be the epitome of that city, and from that I made *Time and Place* (figs. 9, 10, 11). When I did my installation *Lookout/Outlook,* in 1996 and 2009 (fig. 8), it was a culmination of both my time in Eastern Washington camping in fire lookout towers and the time I spent at a residency in Lacoste, France.

Obviously, history is part of my interest in place. Even when younger, when living in California, I read its history. I studied the history of the California Native tribes at Cal. It's as if each piece I make—among other things—asks, *Where am I?* in both time and place.

Maybe because my parents came to NYC from the Midwest, I never felt like there was a specific guidepost. Growing up, everyone I knew was from someplace else, from Italy, Eastern Europe, Sweden, the Caribbean . . . that is what New York is about. So I think I'm always trying to center myself someplace, trying to figure out where I am, and what the stories of the people around me are. It's more than just geographies and histories and time. It's environmental, with a deep concern for the natural world. It is how we fit all that into our lives, how we manage all that now—in our places on this earth.

Lanny Frances DeVuono is an artist, an art writer, and an Associate Professor Emerita at the University of Colorado, Denver. She has received numerous awards for her work, including a Fulbright Fellowship, an Artist Trust Fellowship, a GAP Grant, and residency awards at Yaddo, Centrum, Jentel, RedLine, and the Sitka Center for Art and Ecology, among others.

Lanny DeVuono writes on contemporary art under the name Frances DeVuono. Over the years, she has written for ARTnews, New Art Examiner, Arts Magazine, Artweek, Sculpture magazine, *and* Art in America, *among others. She currently writes for* Third Text *online.*

Expedition, from the series *Polarities: Patterns in Time: 1880/2016, 2.3 Degrees Fahrenheit*, 2016, screenprint and acrylic on panel, 24 × 24 inches, courtesy of the artist and the Augen Gallery.

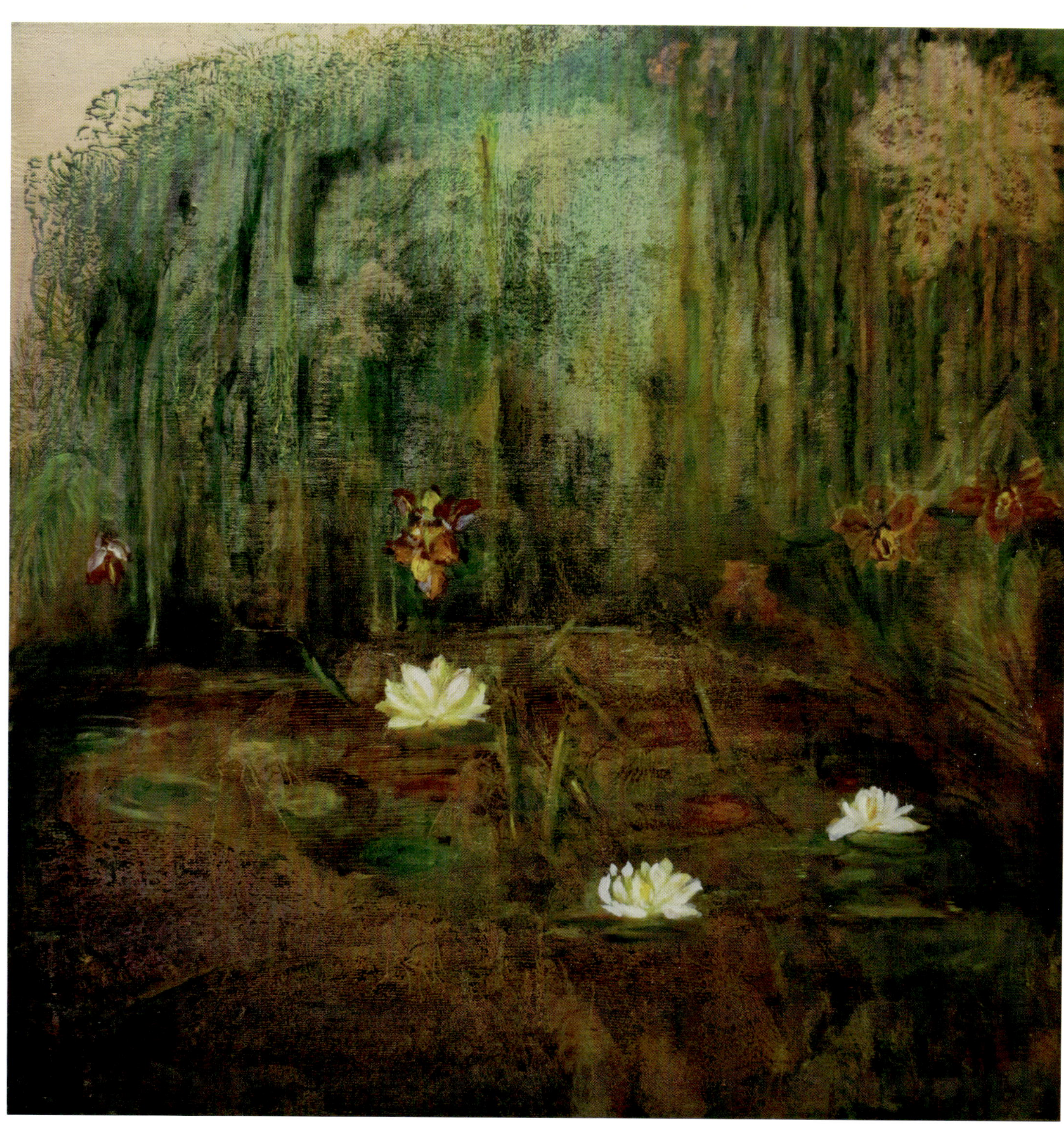

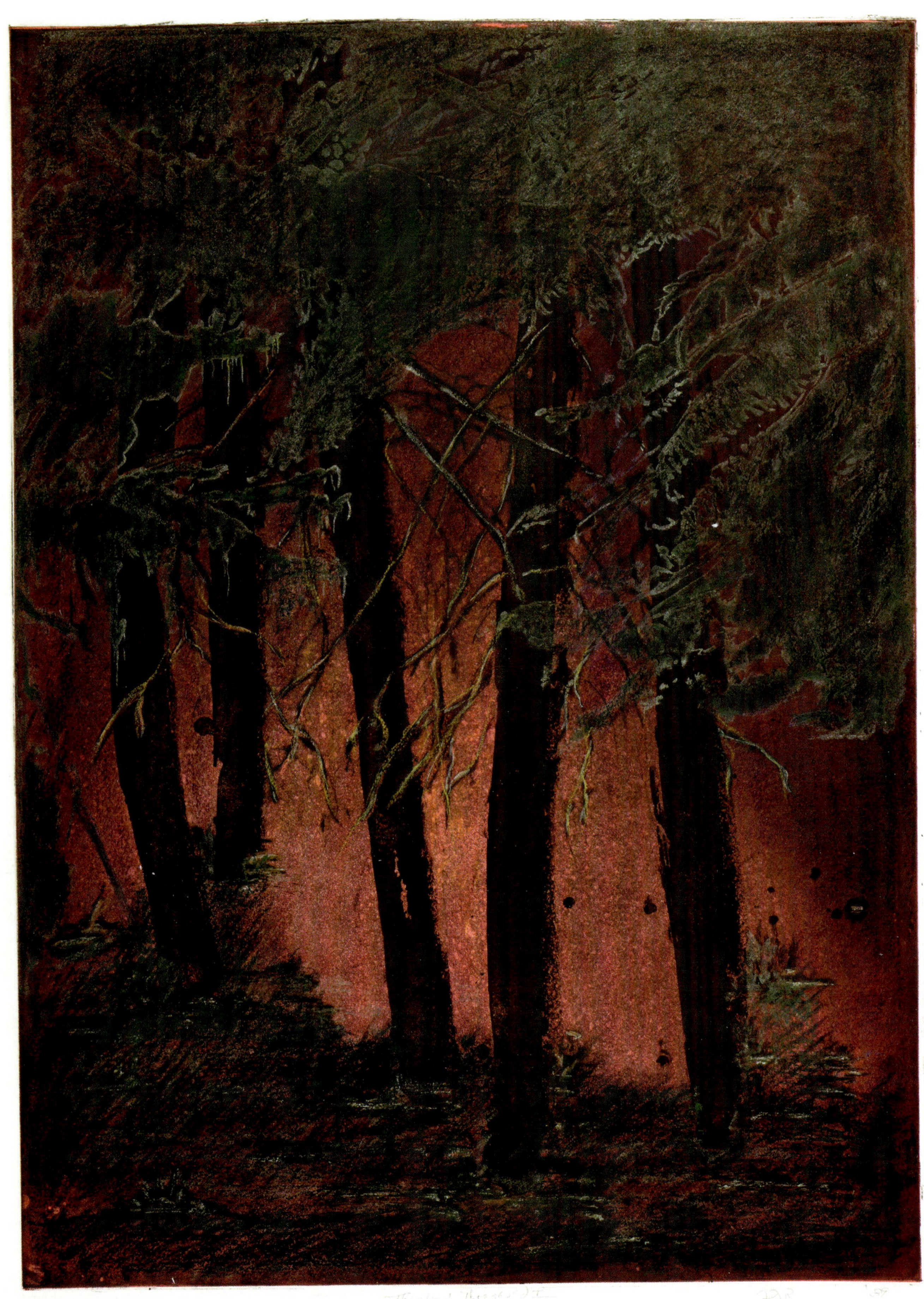

Rita Robillard: The Pullman Years, 1986–1998

Patricia Grieve Watkinson

The chief reason you might come to the small, remote town of Pullman—and stay—is its university. Washington State University accounts for over three quarters of Pullman's citizenry. The town lies among the folds of the undulating Palouse landscape, a sparsely populated and mostly treeless open prairie planted in wheat, barley, and lentils and extending for hundreds of miles across the eastern reaches of the state of Washington.

Naturally, most transplants to Pullman bring with them part of their old lives. Sometimes that element might even grow in significance viewed against the quiet agricultural backdrop of the Palouse hills. Arriving in 1986 to teach art at the university, Rita Robillard brought with her a New York City childhood, a graduate art degree from Cal Berkeley, experience as a graphic designer, several stints teaching at universities in California, and a fascination with trees.[1]

During her early Pullman years, even though she lived in this landscape with its vast stretches of green, gold, and yellow grain, trees remained the focus of Robillard's artwork. The work is a continuation of a passion born in California, most memorably in the Sierra Nevada, where she had frequently hiked and backpacked. Experiences and sensations recollected—walking in forests, encountering forest fires, or sitting by the campfire in the twilight listening to the sounds of nature—sustained her Pullman art practice and perhaps her spirits.

A series of large oil paintings, *Thicket/Threshold* (1984–87), her earliest work in Pullman, reflects expressly those twilight moments. Large, somber tree trunks loom against a darkening night sky (fig. 5). Some of the works are so dark that, as in nature, the viewer's eye takes time to adjust. Other works have areas of silvery glow, as if an unseen moon is casting almost imperceptible shadows and throwing the trees into slight relief. The works are atmospheric, mysterious, and emotive.

The trees here, and in subsequent works, both paintings and mixed-media prints (fig. 31), are not viewed en masse or from a distance. These are not paintings *of* a forest but *in* a forest, close up and intimate. Robillard's trees are individualized and unidealized creations. Invariably, she chooses to show a central section of each tree, with both the crown and the roots omitted. Dead branches, like those on the lower parts of healthy evergreens, are captured with a few deft strokes of the oil stick. The solid forms of tree trunks become strong and rhythmic verticals, juxtaposed with the evanescent areas of moonlight, or sometimes with

Fig. 31: *Thicket/Threshold I*, from the series *Thicket/Threshold*, 1989, monoprint on paper, 30 × 22½ inches, collection of the artist.

suggestions of smoke, water, or the reddish orange of fire. The matte surface of tree bark is contrasted with areas polished to a satiny, reflective surface.

In a following series titled *Pillar* (1988–91), the rhythmic quality of the tree trunks is elaborated on still further, as individual, and almost branchless, trees are depicted in a variety of dance-like poses and gestures (fig. 32). This is as close as Robillard gets to suggesting human forms in the trees. The dancing trunks are definitely female, and they appear both solo and in groupings. Dance depends on gesture, rhythm, and pattern—each a quality intrinsic to Robillard's art. It is not insignificant that dancing is an important means of self-expression for the artist, who is also the daughter of a musician. In addition, Robillard has studied dance in other cultures, notably in Brazil, where she lived for several years.

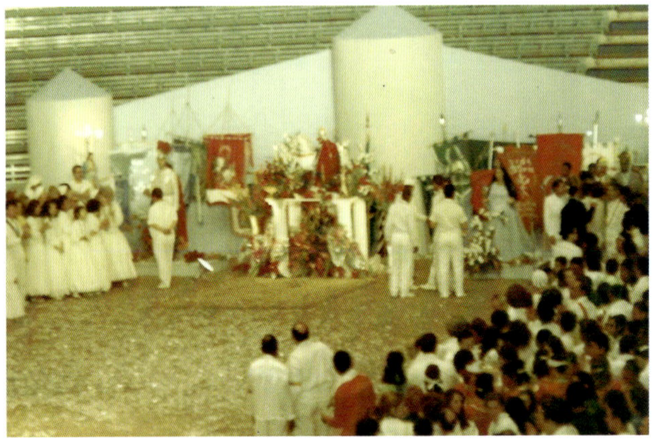

Festival Macumba in São Paulo, Brazil, 1971.

For Robillard, research into areas of knowledge beyond art plays a vital role in informing her work. Historical documents, photographs, vintage books, and contemporary authors are all among her sources. In Brazil, for example, she studied not only traditional dance but also native stories and Afro-Brazilian religions. She has delved deeply into the significance of trees in other cultures and other eras. In ancient Greece, for example, the practice of phyllomancy intrigued her: the voices of rustling leaves were perceived as messages from the gods. In the Celtic world, a complex mythology about sacred trees included the use of tree names to represent letters of Ireland's Ogham alphabet. Robillard uses these names as titles for some of her works: *Tinne* (holly) and *Muinn* (vine).

The worship and celebration of trees through the ages clearly resonate with Robillard's own experience and discovery of nature. For her, like for those before her, trees hold deep and venerable meanings. They are rich in symbolism, be it about an annual cycle of decay and revival, about life and death, or about protection and rootedness. She describes growing up in New York City with little contact with or understanding of nature: out her bedroom window she saw only a series of brick walls, no sky, no sun. Then, in her early twenties, she found herself in rural Brazil with her young family, and for the first time experienced the astounding riches of the natural world. There were orchids growing in trees and butterflies emerging from chrysalises. This ignited her lifelong interest as an amateur naturalist. Later, equally important were her first days and nights spent in the forests of the Californian Sierras that left a deep impression on her psyche, as she shared the ground itself with ancient, magnificent trees.

Fig. 32: *Pillar Ever After*, from the series *Pillars*, 1991, acrylic on panel, 48 × 72 inches, current whereabouts unknown.

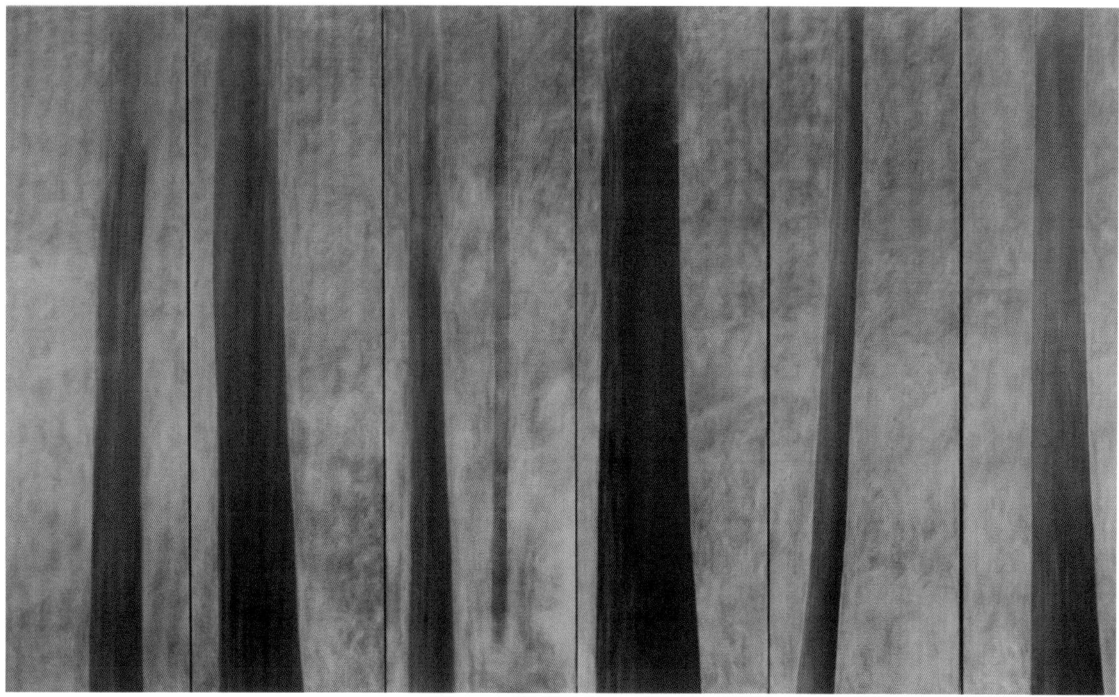

In 1990, Robillard was accepted for a summer residency at Dorland Mountain Arts Colony in California. This gave her the opportunity to begin a new series of prints, in part inspired by the indigenous live oaks of the area. She says, "I tried to capture the mystery and the moment of being in a grove of trees, the simultaneous experience of shifts of light, the rustling of the leaves, and the gestures of the trunks." The works, which have a strong graphic sensibility, feature tree limbs on a dark background with an inset central "window" of another, more colorful and detailed close-up of a tree. The background is a negative, high-contrast image from a photograph: the collaged central image is positive and originates from a drawing. The tension between the two very textural images sets up a dynamic relationship that emphasizes the dancing forms and the sense of rhythmic pattern.

This *Windows* (1991) series, which Robillard thinks may refer to the viewless window of her childhood, is a good example of the artist's characteristically multilayered approach to working (fig. 33). The techniques involved are surprisingly complex. The photography is processed through several generations of media, using a Xerox machine to break down the image, which is printed on Kodalith film to give a very dense black. Photolithography is used as well as water-based photo-screenprinting. Each print is collaged, then finally hand-colored and drawn on. The prints are not editioned: printing techniques are employed solely to provide the visual effects Robillard desires. She is not in the least interested in a mass-produced image.

Windows was Robillard's first opportunity to use screenprinting and nontoxic, water-based inks—a significant step in her career as an artist and an academic. When hired to teach printmaking and graphic design at Washington State University, she was already aware of the health risks of traditional screenprinting with its hazardous solvents and inks. Her good

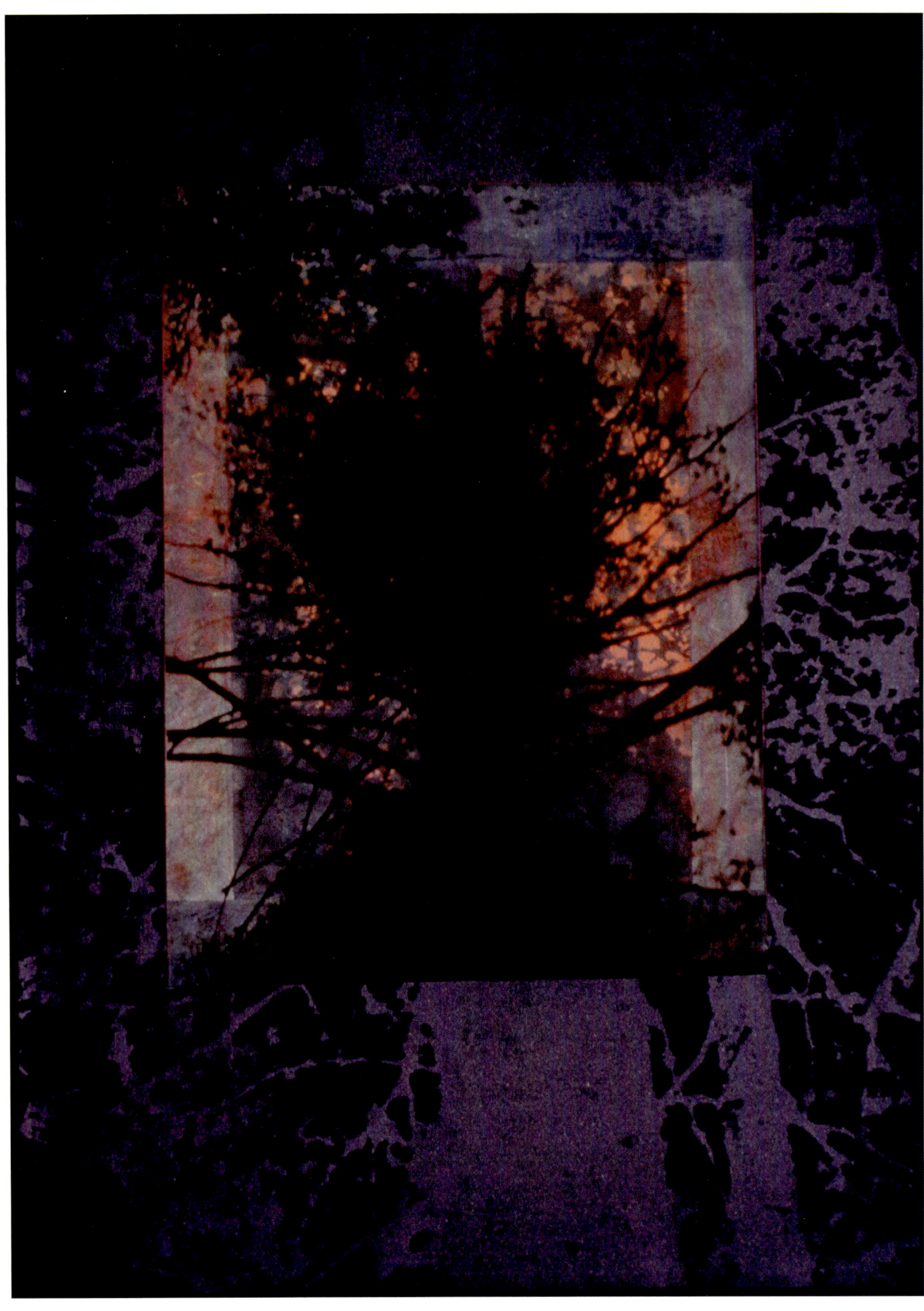

friend and inspiring art professor Sylvia Lark had died young,[2] perhaps from these toxins. Robillard quickly gained university support to transform the printmaking studios into a safe environment and to introduce the first use of digital media. In the process, she taught herself about the new techniques and materials: she took special delight in acrylics from Golden Artist Colors, Inc.,[3] which could be used for painting or printmaking and came in vibrant colors and iridescents.

With her knowledge about safe printmaking, Robillard was often invited to speak on the subject. In 1991, the College Art Association asked her and her colleague, artist Jo Hockenhull, to propose a panel for the annual meeting. Robillard decided to augment her presentation with a series of prints that addressed toxicity at a much greater level—a global level. At issue was the disposal of nuclear waste. Having lived in Pullman for five years by this point, Robillard— a longtime member of SANE (National Committee for a Sane Nuclear Policy)—had become all too aware she was a mere one hundred miles downwind from Hanford, the vast industrial complex that manufactured plutonium used in World War II and throughout the Cold War. The most contaminated nuclear site in the USA, Hanford had radioactive waste—some with a half-life of thousands or millions of years—that stymied scientists and politicians alike. Basing her work on a publication by the Union of Concerned Scientists, Robillard focused on the absurd or unimaginable suggestions the book debunks. Posing the question "What can be done with nuclear waste?" she created *Votives for Hanford*, a series of twenty-five screenprints using the lush, vibrant colors that the new screenprinting inks provided.

Although *Votives* (1990) uses print media, each work is unique, with hand coloring and collage. Jewellike colors, iridescent and richly textured backgrounds, and collaged elements make for intricate and layered effects (fig. 7). Brightly colored angels—appropriated from Giotto and Fra Angelico—wring their hands as they hover over rows of isotopes or deceptively joyous orange barrels of waste storage. (The diagrams of isotopes were made in collaboration with the Washington State University Department of Physics.) Robillard presents this threat that is both invisible and beyond human comprehension. The angels are witness to our human folly (fig. 34). A written statement, culled from news media or from scientific writings, accompanies each work and emphasizes that the folly has no end: there's a suggestion to transport the radioactive waste out of our solar system by rocket and another to bury it deep in the earth's crust, under the ocean!

Votives is an instance where Robillard chooses to include contemporary political issues in her art. A politically engaged individual, she mostly keeps her art and her politics separate, believing that art is unlikely to be an effective change agent. While reviewers have seen her focus on trees as a lament for the environment or an indictment of the logging industry, she rejects the interpretations. Even in *Votives*, dealing with a subject matter of horrendous implications, Robillard declines a dystopic response, aiming instead to create works that

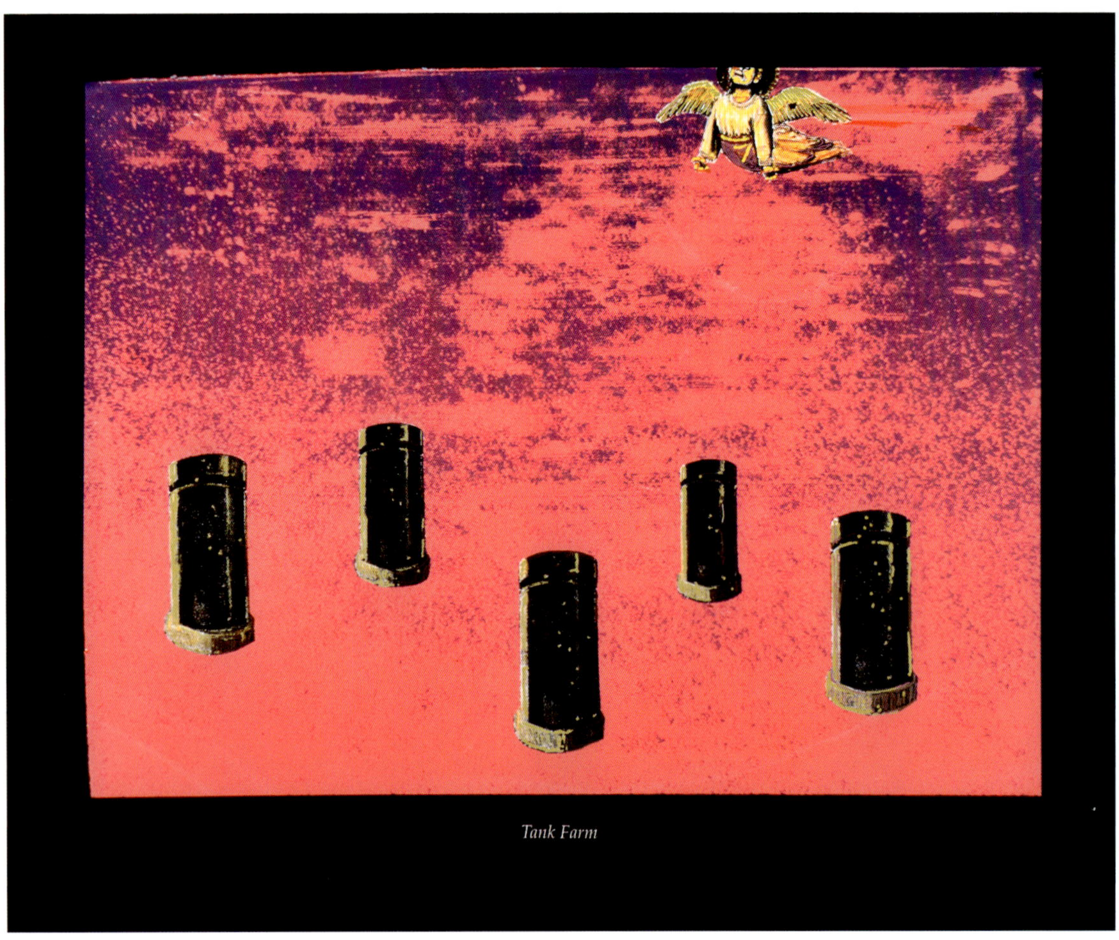

Tank Farm

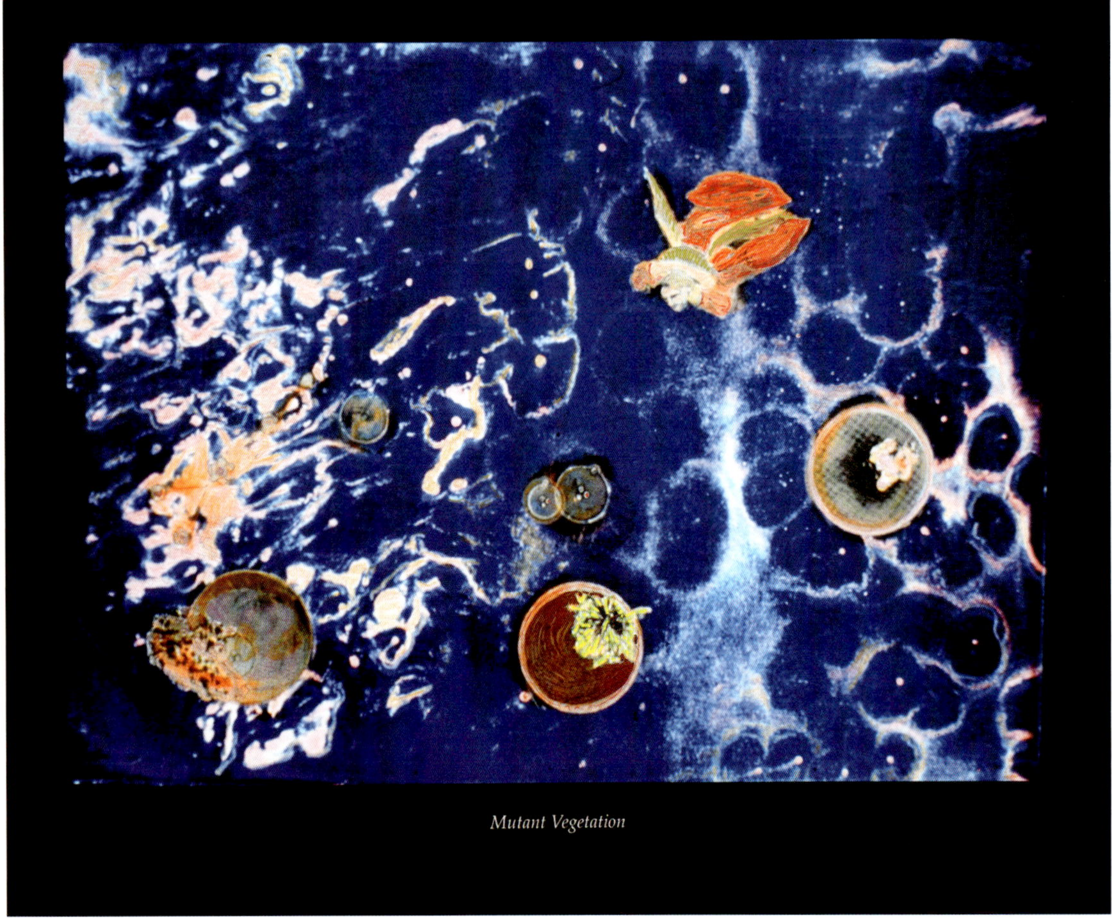

Mutant Vegetation

Fig. 34: *Tank Farm*, from the series *Votives for Hanford*, 1990–96, revised in 2019–20, pigment print mounted on panel, 16 × 20 inches, courtesy of the artist and the Augen Gallery.

Fig. 35: *Mutant Vegetation*, from the series *Votives for Hanford*, 1990–96, revised in 2019–20, pigment print mounted on panel, 16 × 20 inches, courtesy of the artist and the Augen Gallery.

are both beautiful and insightful (fig. 35). This is an important aspect of her approach to art . . . and to life. While not overtly feminist in her art making, Robillard is nevertheless very conscious of being a woman and an artist, of making aesthetic decisions that are not about telling others how to think or behave, but of choosing to devote herself to a personal practice that, first and foremost, gives her—and hopefully others— visual pleasure.

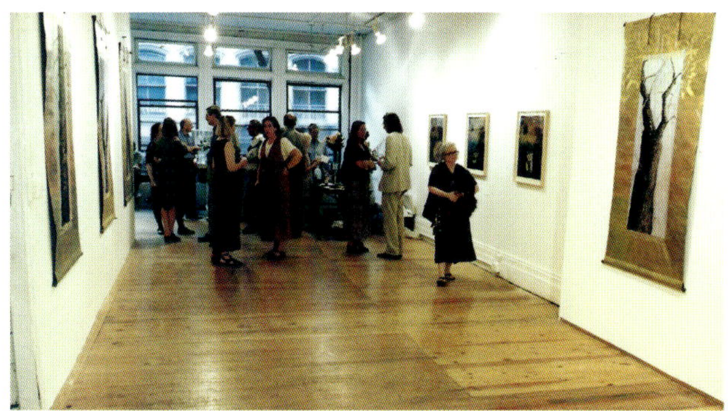

Opening of the exhibition *The Garden, the Park, and the Fall from Grace* at the A.I.R. Gallery, New York City, 1997.

Soon, however, trees resumed center stage in Robillard's work. This time they were found on her own doorstep in Pullman—a cluster of cottonwoods, self-sown along the Palouse River. The series *Cottonwoods of the Palouse* (1993–95) employed a new format— scrolls reminiscent of Chinese or Japanese art; Robillard has been a serious student of Asian art. The choice of presentation glorifies these common yet iconic trees of the American West (fig. 6). At the center of each scroll, bare, dark tree trunks are rendered in oil stick, their individualized postures stark against what seems to be a luminous dawn or evening sky in pure shades of pink, purple, yellow, and blue (fig. 36). The surrounding surfaces of the scroll are sumptuous in their effect: layers of faint, printed imagery are overlaid with metallic gold paint that shines like a rich brocade. These shimmering, light-filled works capture Robillard's awareness of the special quality of light characteristic of the Palouse as well as the gold of the ripened wheat fields and what she has called "the texture of place."

By this time, Robillard had discovered the plentiful forests of Idaho, whose western border is just a short drive from Pullman. In that area, the soil and climate support vigorous conifers, and designated wilderness areas are interspersed with stands of timber for logging. Fire lookout towers have been a feature of the region since the early twentieth century, although their use is declining drastically. These hilltop towers, with their panoramic and distant views, intrigued Robillard and found an echo in another experience—she had spent an art residency in the hilltop town of Lacoste, France, where the castle, once occupied by the Marquis de Sade, had a similar 360-degree overview of the surrounding landscape. Uniting the two experiences, quite distinct in time and place, Robillard created *Lookout/Outlook* (1993–94). It is an ambitious twenty-eight-foot-long, three-foot-high print installation that wraps continuously and seamlessly around a gallery (fig. 8). The background of the work incorporates low-resolution imagery from photographs of the French town's medieval stone walls and is printed in iridescent inks. Added to this, collaged on, are twenty-eight "windows" that surround the viewer (fig. 37). In each, there are computer-manipulated photographs of dramatic skies as if seen from a lookout tower in Idaho. Sunsets, sunrises, and storms are so fiery in their heightened coloration that the forest might truly be on fire.

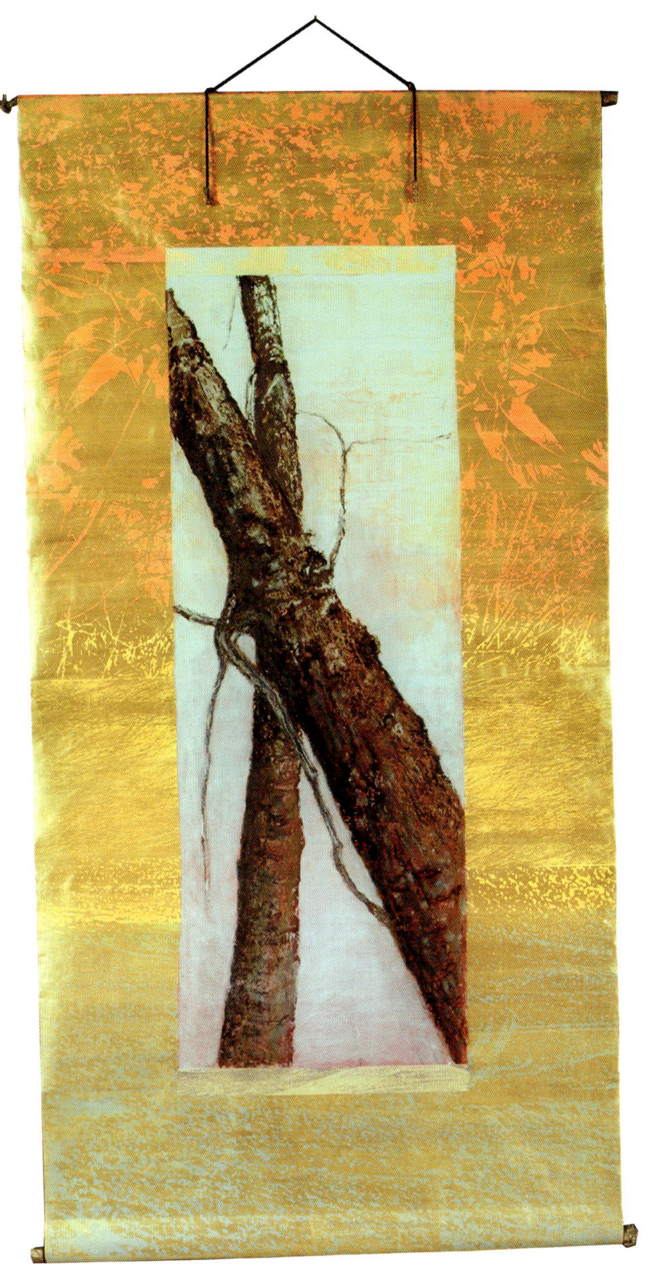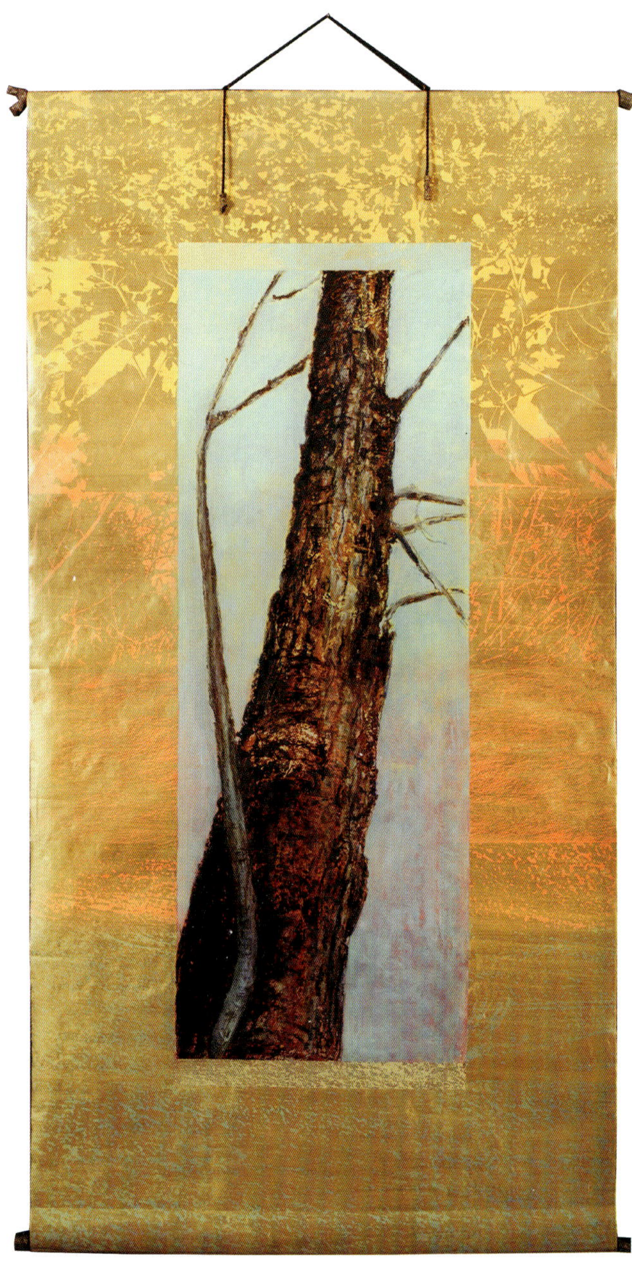

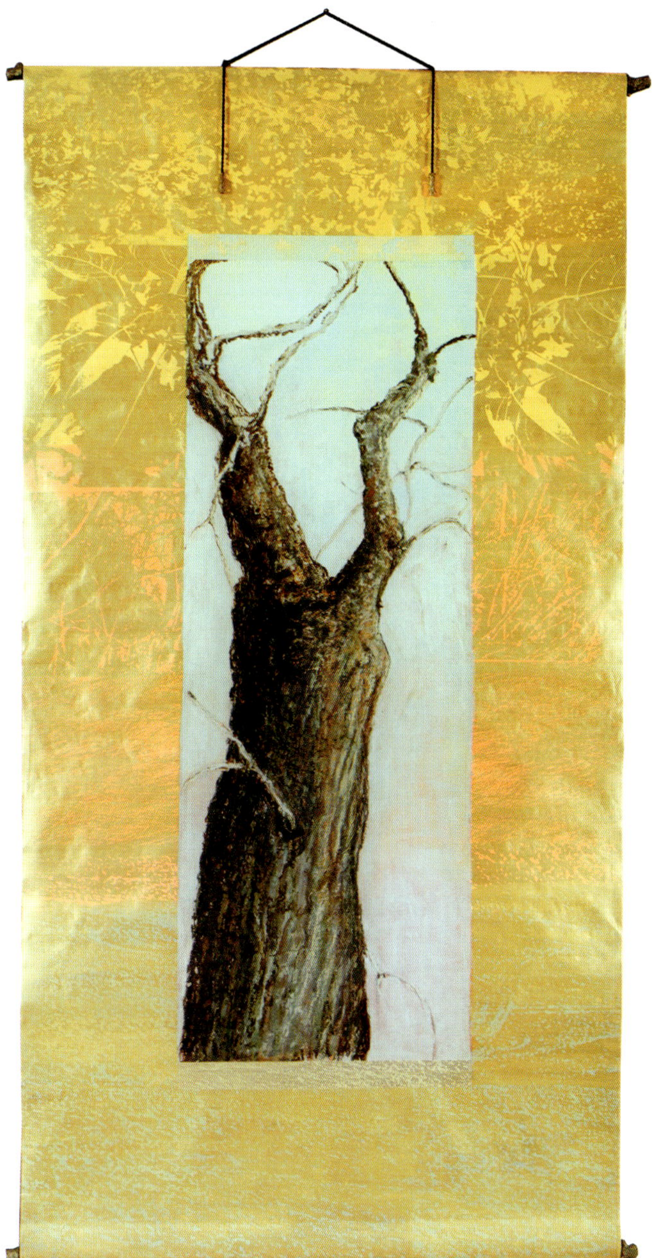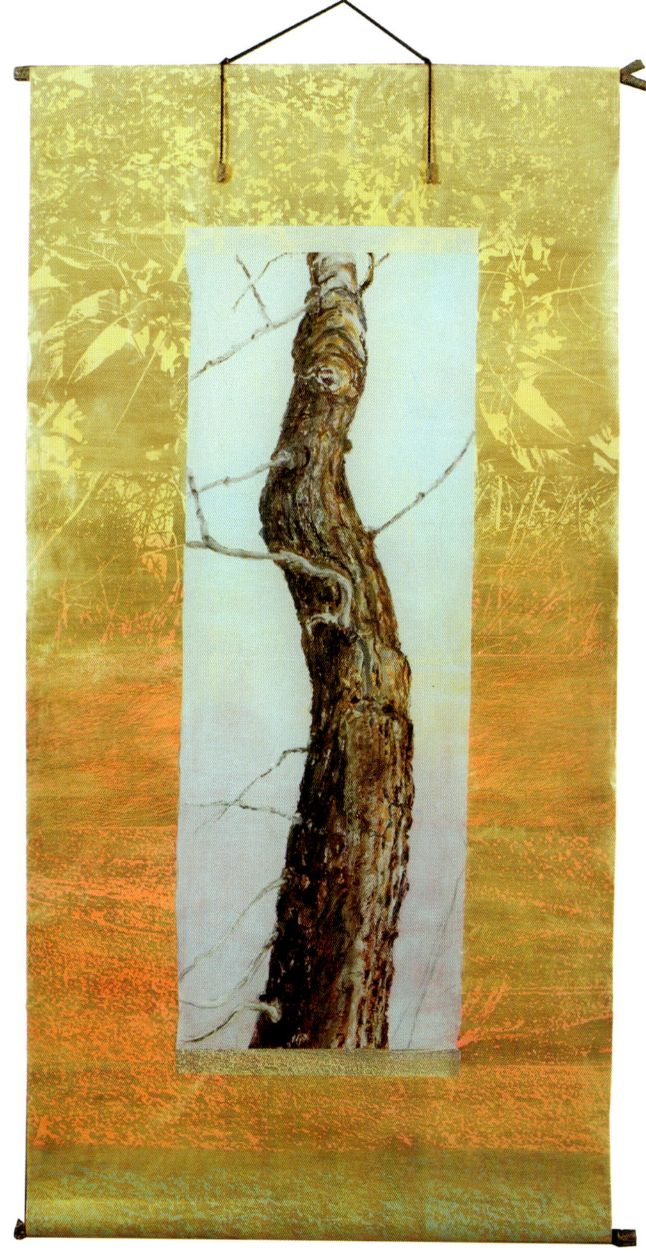

Fig. 36: *Cottonwoods of the Palouse*, 1993–95, screenprint, acrylic, and oil sticks on gampi or mulberry paper mounted on Tyvek, 72 × 36 inches each, collection of the artist.

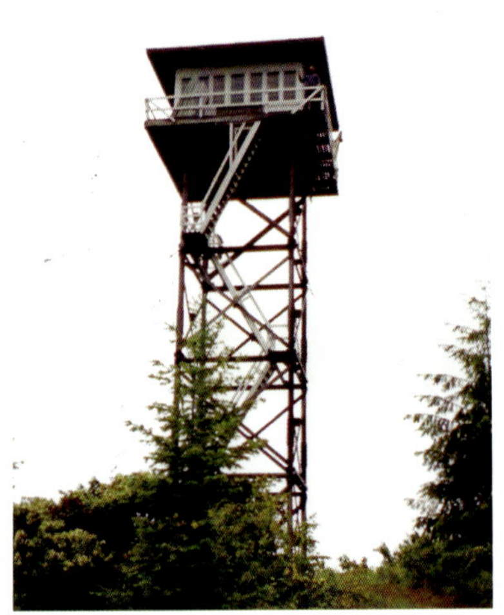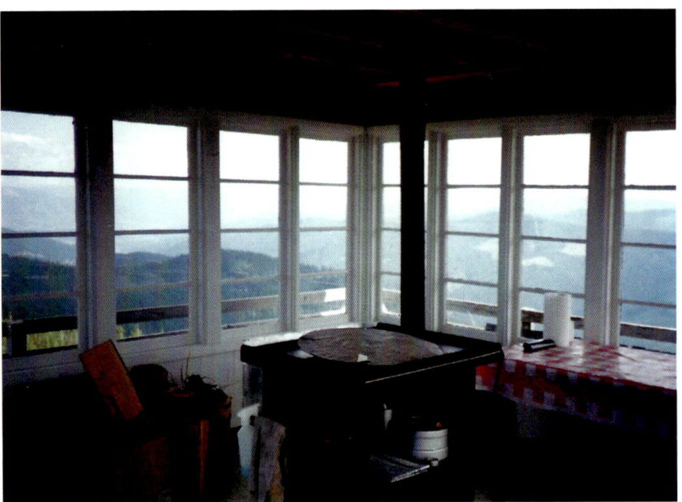

For Robillard, this work is a metaphor for "the danger of seeing what you are looking for." *Lookout/Outlook* is a notable departure from previous Pullman work: Robillard's intimate focus on trees has given way to a distant vista. Here she looks outward—*over*, not *into*, the forest. Perhaps not coincidentally, Robillard now begins to move away from her close involvement with trees.

These were Robillard's final Pullman years: she left in 1998 to chair the art department at Portland State University in neighboring Oregon. Her major work in the period before leaving was a series of twenty mixed-media prints, *Essence and Artifice: Views of Spokane* (1996–98). The largest city in Washington's "Inland Empire," Spokane is a seventy-five-mile drive north of Pullman. That Robillard would choose to focus on a city as her subject matter, beginning a visual investigation quite different from her previous work, suggests she was more than ready for a change. Indeed, this new approach ultimately carried her forward into her future life and career.

Essence and Artifice presents a layered meaning of place—one of Robillard's central concerns. She credits Spokane gallery owner Lorinda Knight with opening her eyes to the intricacies and idiosyncrasies of the city.[4] The work is about Robillard's understanding of the past and how it influences the present. In Spokane, once the home of Indigenous tribes, then of trappers, loggers, and miners, she finds examples of a city's conscious striving for European antecedents that are nothing short of ironic. Thus the elegant 1914 Davenport Hotel has a "Hall of the Doges" modeled after the fourteenth-century Doge's Palace in Venice (fig. 38). Then there is a park fashioned after Versailles and Roman-like sculptures that adorn a downtown theater. A most telling juxtaposition for Robillard is the 1890 Spokane Club building with a picture of Chief Spokane on its facade and a "Members Only" sign on the door (fig. 39).

As always, these thoughts are translated into works of art that are not didactic but poetically beautiful and gentle as they convey the artist's message. The format of a central, collaged image on a textured background is already familiar from earlier work. Robillard continues her

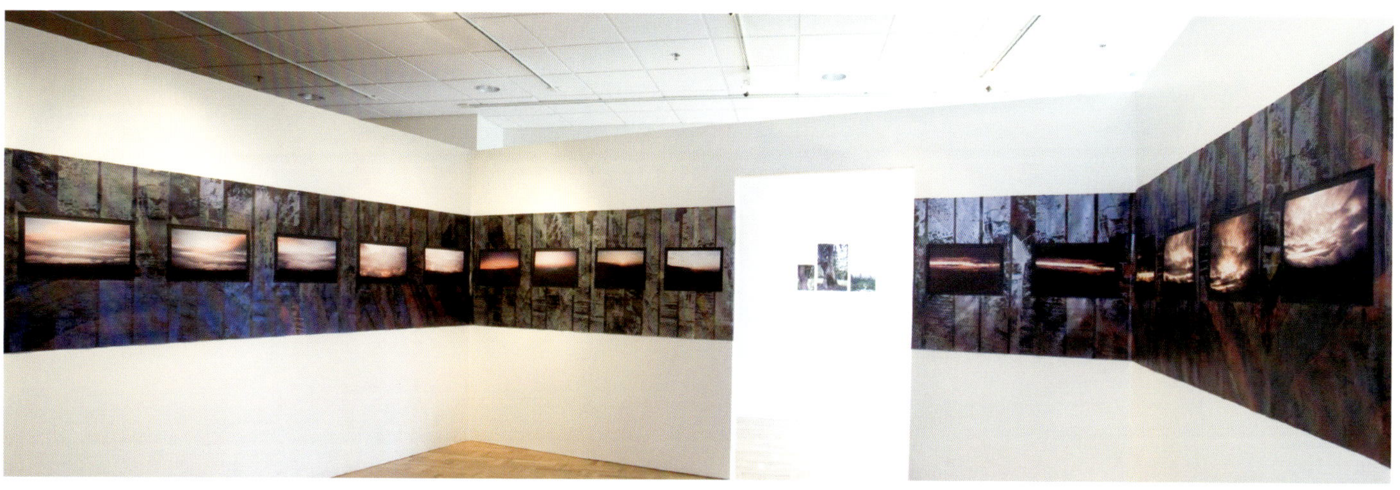

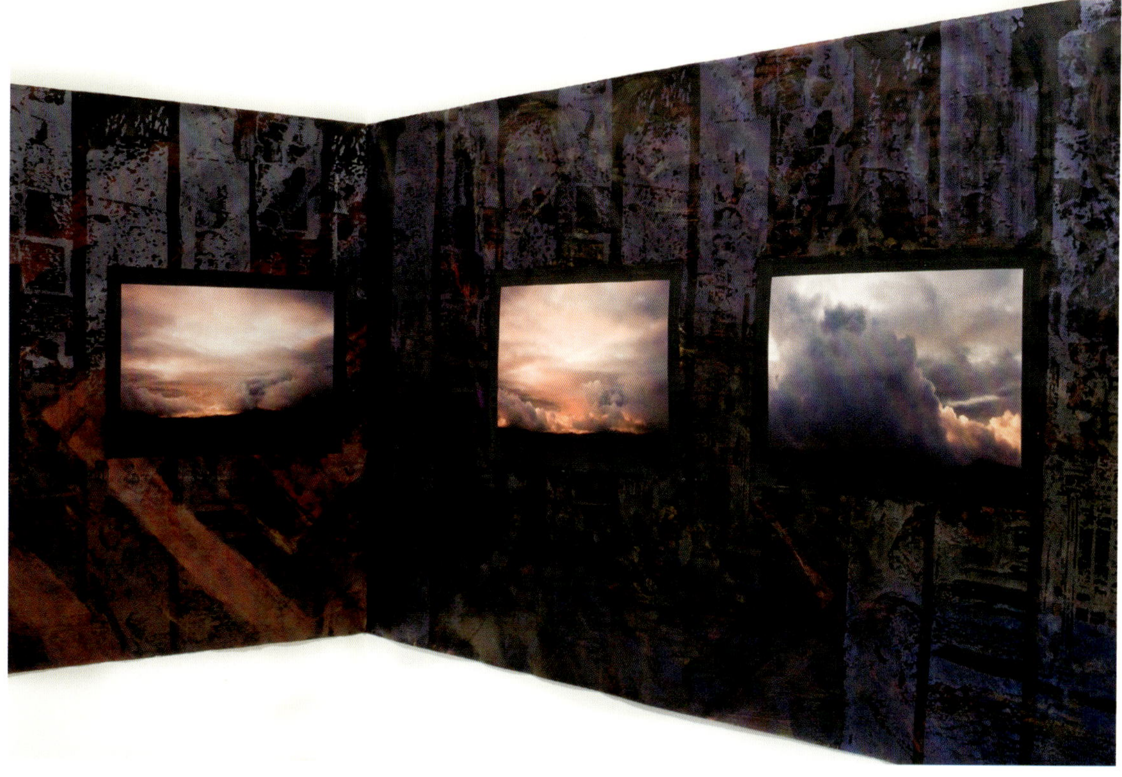

Fig. 37: *Lookout/Outlook*, installation views, 1996–2009, digital photographs mounted on Tyvek, 28 prints, 36 × 20 inches each, collection of the artist.

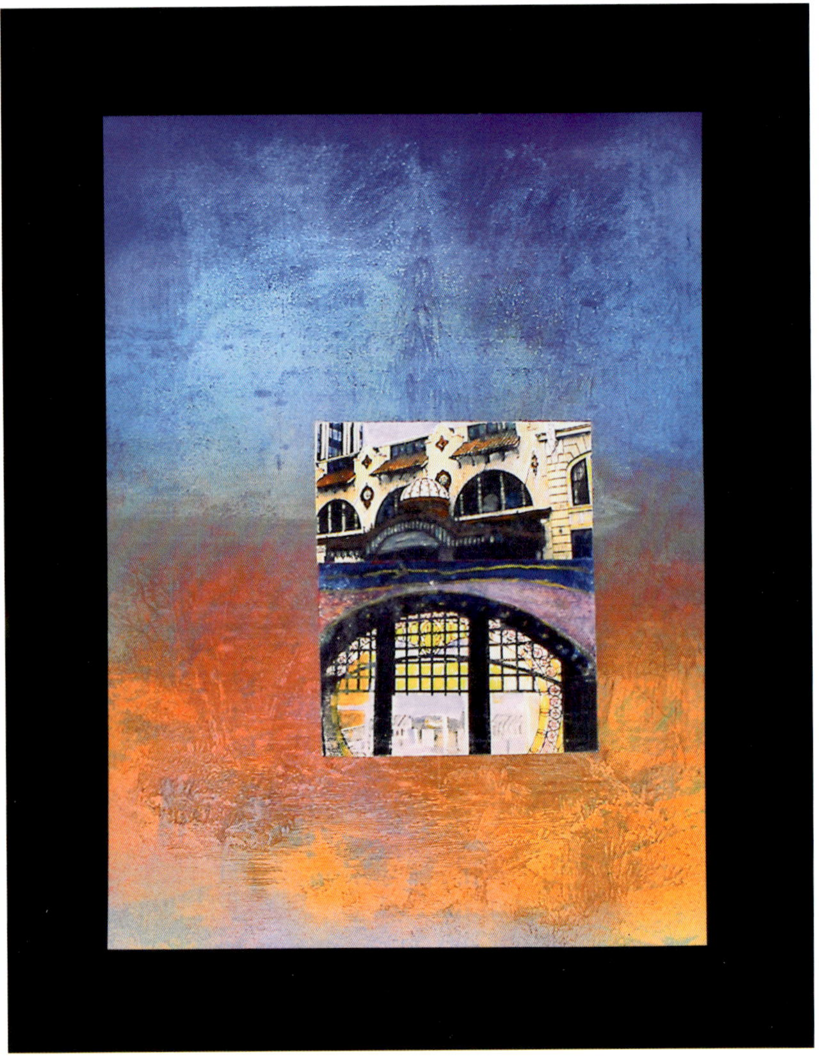

exploration of color and finds her stride as a colorist with glorious shades and vivid passages, often enhanced by her much-loved iridescent pigments. There is a visual splendor to these works that seems more joyous, more emotional, than intellectual or conceptual. Yet with Robillard, intellectual underpinnings are never far away . . . the intriguing filigreed textures of the backgrounds come from greatly enlarged engravings culled from her trove of vintage travel books. Ironically, of course, these are mostly nineteenth-century European volumes replete with idealized landscapes, often a source of inspiration for New World urban planners. Each collaged central image was one she photographed in present-day Spokane, and yet each is presented as if it were a hand-colored nineteenth-century photograph. Thus elements of time itself are hidden in the very making of the artwork.

There is a further dimension to *Essence and Artifice*, the culmination of Robillard's Pullman years. In exploring the European cultural symbols of a western American city, Robillard might also be examining her own interests as an artist. She recognizes her heritage as part of a northern European artistic tradition: she looks to the Romantic nineteenth-century landscape artists and not to the New York School or the Abstract Expressionists. She embraces ideas about place, landscape, environment, and ecology. She cites a wide range of artists who have

Fig. 38: *Davenport, Palace of the Doges*, from the series *Essence and Artifice: Views of Spokane*, 1998–2020, digital print on paper, 20 × 16 inches, collection of the artist.

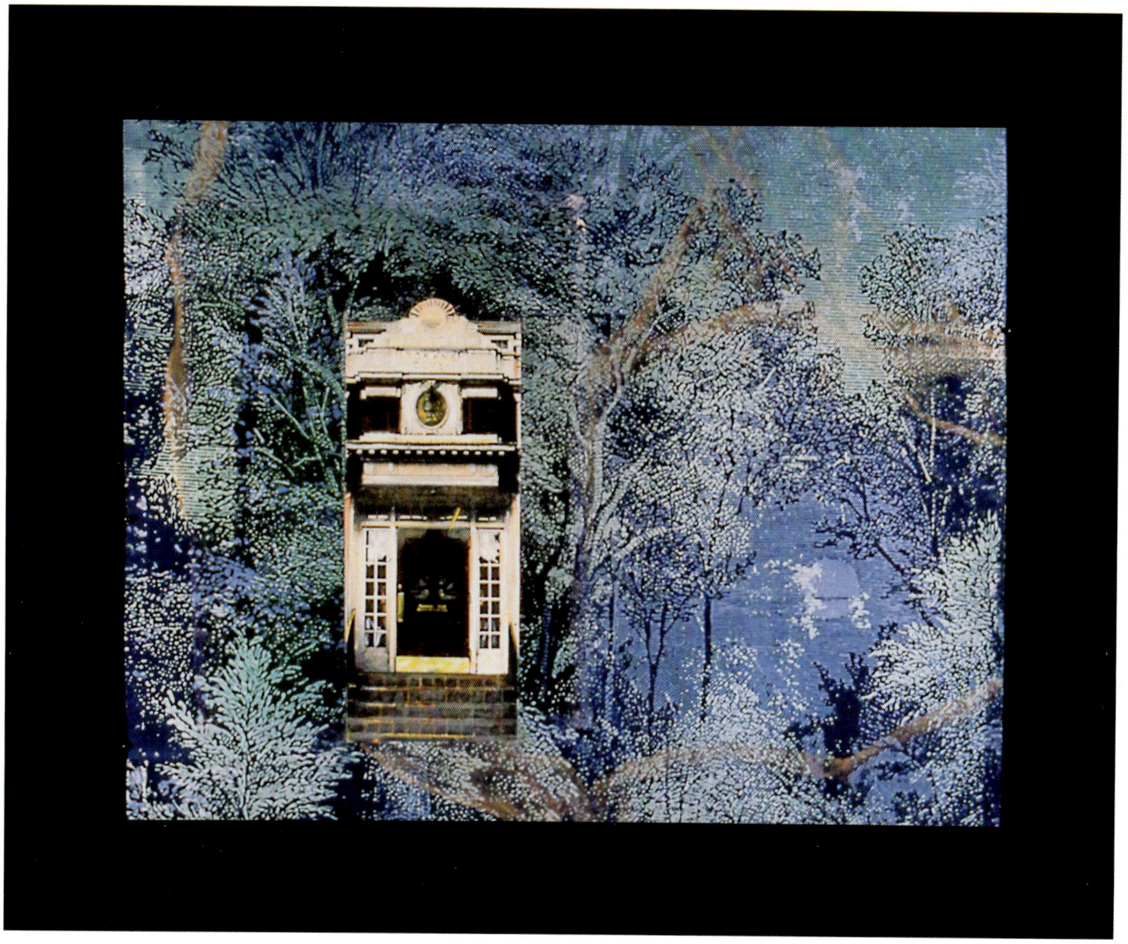

influenced her: the nineteenth-century landscapes of George Inness, Thomas Cole, and John Kensett; the quest for nature's essence in the works of Arthur Dove, Morris Graves, and Georgia O'Keeffe; the countless contemporary artists concerned with environmental issues; the use of pattern and color by Miriam Schapiro and the quest for beauty by Ciel Bergman—both with feminist concerns. In the end, it is Robillard's unique use of technique and media in service of her intellectual inquiry and expressed in creations of visual beauty that form the legacy of this period of her life—the Pullman years.

Patricia Grieve Watkinson is an essayist on the art and artists of the Pacific Northwest. She is the former director of the Museum of Art at Washington State University, the Fort Wayne Museum of Art in Indiana, and Pilchuck Glass School in Washington State.

Notes

Fig. 39: *Members Only*, from the series *Essence and Artifice: Views of Spokane*, 1998–2020, digital print on paper, 16 × 20 inches, collection of the artist.

1 The author spent time interviewing Robillard and making studio visits during 2018. Unattributed quotes by the artist date from that time.

2 Sylvia Lark (1947–1990) was a painter, printmaker, curator, and educator who taught at the University of California, Berkeley, where Rita Robillard was one of her students.

3 Golden Artist Colors, Inc., of New Berlin, New York.

4 Lorinda Knight operated the Lorinda Knight Gallery in Spokane from 1996 until 2009.

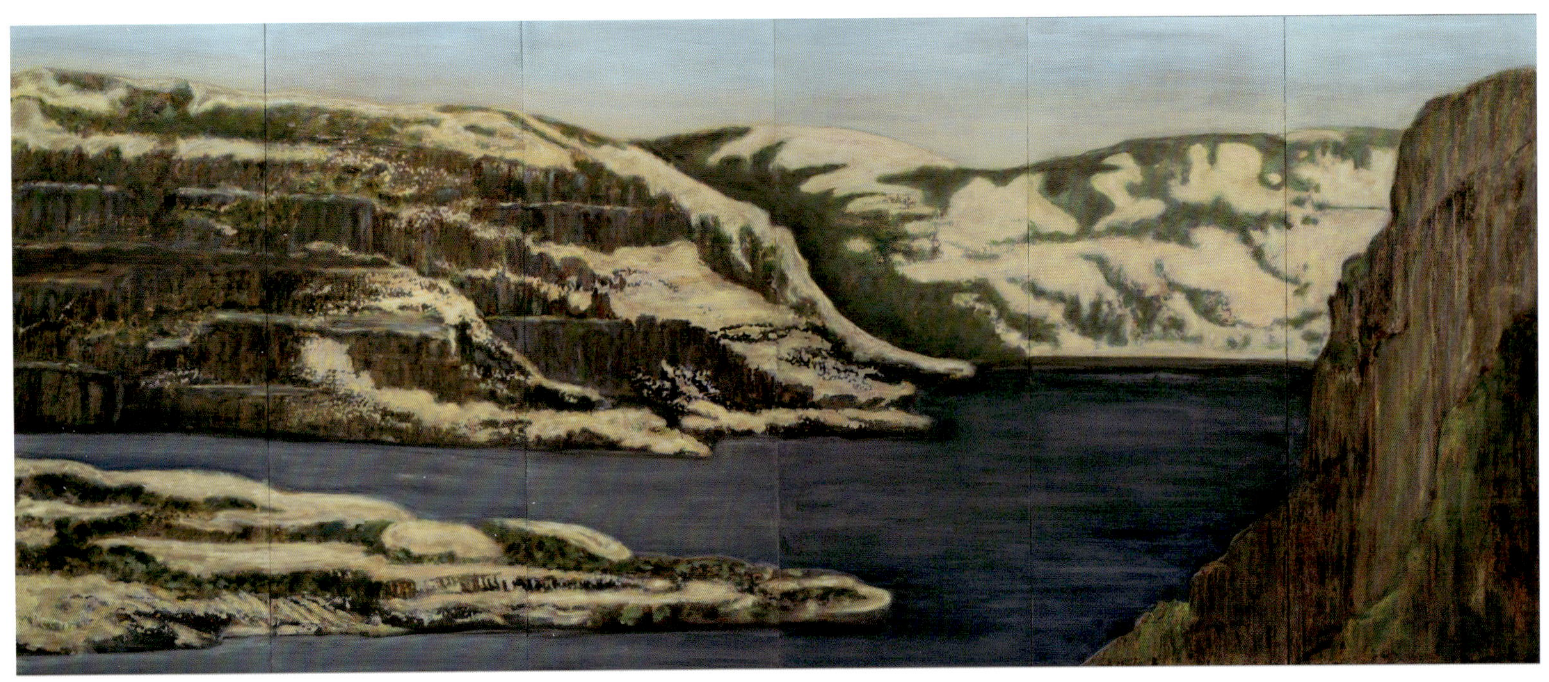

Rita Robillard: The Portland Years, 1998–Present

Linda Tesner

A constant through line in Rita Robillard's career—a line that in fact weaves through her entire life—is that she is an inveterate explorer. She is deeply curious about her environment and inquisitive about how history—cultural, political, social, geological—have left indelible marks on the landscape she inhabits. She has lived and traveled widely, so her life experiences have provided deep and rich source material. Her inquiries have led to scholarly research and innumerable relationships with other academics whose work correlates to Robillard's. This incessant curiosity informs her studio practice, and invariably, her artwork. Robillard's oeuvre is a chronicle of her most serious interrogations; *Rita Robillard: Time and Place* illustrates her abundant answers.

> *We shall not cease from exploration / And the end of all our exploring / Will be to arrive where we started / And know the place for the first time.*
>
> T. S. Eliot, "Little Gidding"[1]

When Robillard accepted the position of chair at the department of art at Portland State University in 1998, she relocated from Pullman, Washington, to Portland, Oregon. Her move transported her from the fertile, rolling hills of the Palouse in the southeasternmost corner of Washington, where she taught in the fine arts department of Washington State University from 1986 until 1998, and transplanted her to an urban center, Portland, a bustling midsize city. From Pullman to Portland, Robillard followed the route traveled by the Corps of Discovery along the Columbia River toward the Pacific Ocean.

Robillard's painting *The Gorge*, now called *Nch'i-Wána (Columbia River), 1860–2021* (2021) visualizes her journey from the Palouse to the Willamette Valley (fig. 40). "Nch'i-Wána" means "the big river," and this seven-foot painting depicts the Columbia Gorge, in the general region of The Dalles, Oregon, the area archaically known as *"les dalles"* for the columnar basalt rocks carved by the river. Lewis and Clark camped near here in 1805; the Columbia River route was originally the only way for pioneers to reach Oregon City and the end of the Oregon Trail.

Fig. 40: *The Gorge*, now called *Nch'i-Wána (Columbia River), 1860–2021*, from the series *Time and Place*, 2001–21, screenprint, acrylic, and oil on panel, 36 × 87 inches, courtesy of the artist and the Augen Gallery.

The title of *Nch'i-Wána* refers to 1860, which provides a clue to the way Robillard works. Her studio output involves many, many layers of additive and subtractive processes. She very often begins with a base appropriated from a vintage illustration. In the case of this painting, Robillard sourced a very small lithograph—only three by four inches—from the Oregon

Historical Society. The identification of the lithograph is "View on the Columbia River, at the Commencement of The Dalles." Remarkably, with the aid of master printer Mark Mahaffey, she enlarged this graphic to the panoramic scale of the painting as a base to guide overlays of screenprint and painting, applying Robillard's own hand—and experiences—to this singular vista. Robillard's view of the Columbia Gorge is a deliberate portrayal of a landscape with centuries-old roots and tremendous historic significance.[2] In Robillard's passage to Portland, the historical became personal.

Robillard's explorer nature was already well established by the time she moved to Portland. She had a deeply rooted love of both landscape and history, of learning the minutiae about wherever she lived, and of reflecting upon her own place within a specific environment. She credits this attentiveness to her youth and early adulthood. Experiences such as going to camp and learning to swim in the Hudson River near Saugerties, New York; living in São Paulo and the rural village of Lagoa Santa in Brazil; then living in Lacoste, France; and backpacking in the Sierra Nevadas—these are just a few of the life experiences that honed Robillard's scrutiny of place. When Robillard arrived in Portland, she immediately marshaled her innate investigative nature and proceeded to study her new city. She had already done a similar project when she lived in Pullman; *Essence and Artifice: Views of Spokane* (1996–98) was a series of twenty mixed-media prints based on the history and architecture of nearby Spokane (figs. 38, 39). Now in Portland, Robillard reached out to thirteen Portlanders and asked them to introduce her to their most beloved and personally significant locations in Portland, places that characterize the spirit of the city.[3] Among these thirteen guides were curators, artists, historians, scientists, a Native American, and food and garden enthusiasts. Robillard joined her docents on flânerie strolls around Portland, taking note of details that piqued her interest. She trained these experiences into a series called *Time and Place*.

Robillard paired her on-the-ground research with fact- and imagine-finding missions at the Oregon Historical Society and Portland State University's Special Collections Library in a quest to pinpoint the quiddities of her new home. She appropriated anonymous images documenting the history of Portland from vintage travel books and historic archives. To these she added her own digital images of specific Portland architectural details in multilayered prints that visually merged the past with the present. *Gilbert 1893* (2001) is an excellent example (fig. 41). Here Robillard overlaid an image of the Gilbert Building at 319 SW Taylor Street in Portland; it was built in 1893. The building was significant to Robillard because, at the time, the Elizabeth Leach Gallery was housed near that building, and Robillard's work was represented there. *Pioneers* (2001) is another example, in which a detail of an ox-drawn wagon on the Oregon Trail is superimposed over an appropriated engraving of a farm family at harvest (fig. 42). The wagon trail detail is taken from the impressive bronze doors of the United States National Bank Building on SW Sixth Avenue downtown

Fig. 41: *Gilbert 1893*, from the series *Time and Place*, 2001, screenprint and digital print on panel, 20 × 20 inches, collection of the artist.

Fig. 42: *Pioneers*, from the series *Time and Place*, 2001, screenprint and digital print on paper, 20 × 20 inches, collection of Deborah and Martin Merkle.

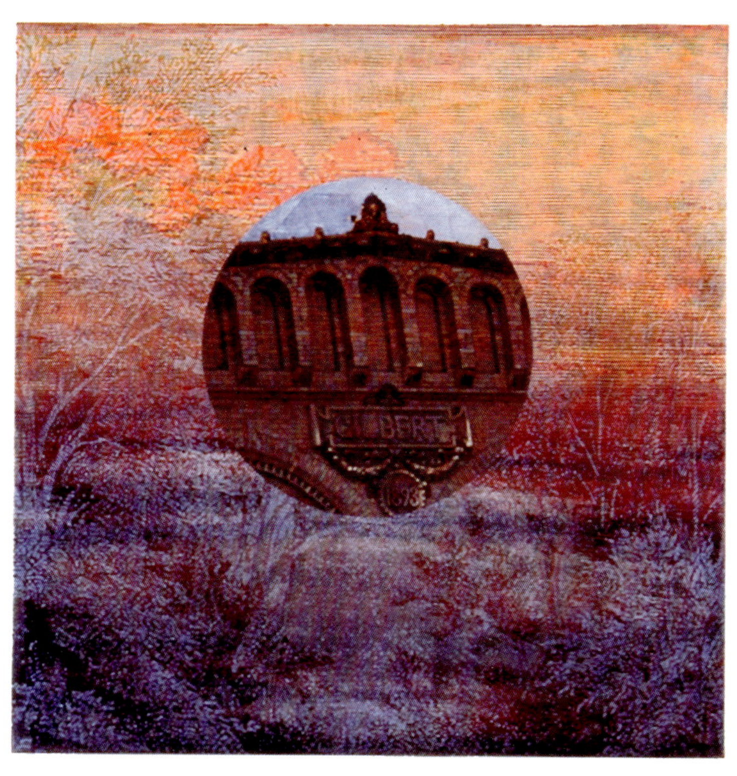

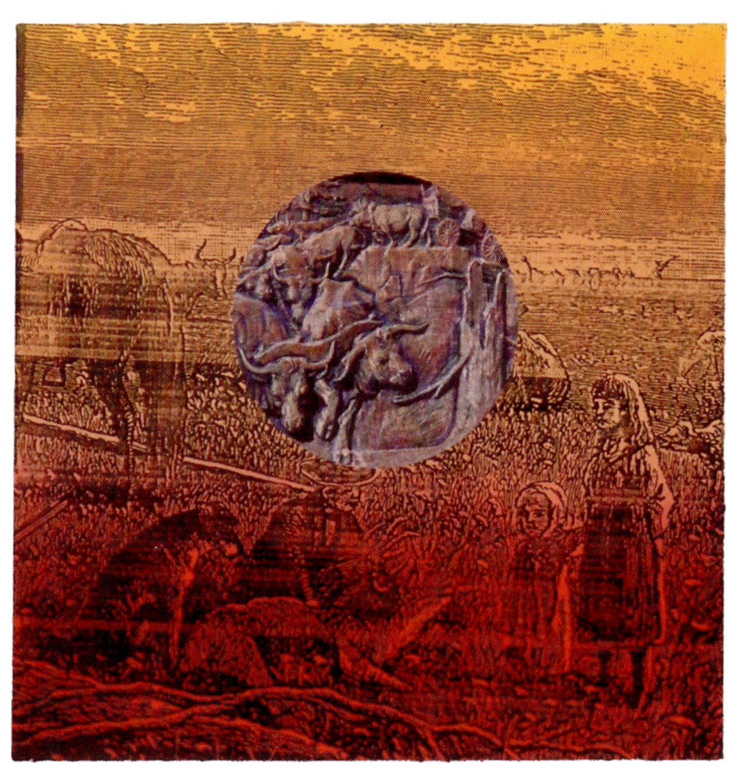

in Portland, itself an important architectural landmark, as the building was designed by A. E. Doyle and is listed on the National Register of Historic Places. The narrative bas-relief panels on the bronze doors were designed by Avard Fairbanks to depict noble aspects of Oregon history. These central images—the Gilbert Building cornerstone, the Fairbanks panel—were transferred into Robillard's hybrid prints/drawings in luminescent iridescent ink, evoking, perhaps, the romanticism of historic landscape paintings, such as those by Albert Bierstadt and Thomas Moran. In the process of this artistic treasure hunt represented by Robillard's process, she familiarized herself with distinctive Portland features and insinuated herself into her new home.

It's important to revisit Robillard's process, as it is quite unusual; it is multi-stepped and idiosyncratic. It begins with photo printmaking, which subtly underscores her respect for the unknown and unacknowledged artists whose illustrations provide such richness in the historical volumes from which she produces her substrate imagery. She begins by printing an appropriated landscape on either panel or paper, then she proceeds to layer in more imagery. While printmaking lays the foundation for the work, Robillard manipulates her surfaces in various ways: by sanding and carving into the layers of pigment and by painting or drawing between and on top of layers of print. Further depth comes from her careful overlays of flat colors against metallic or iridescent hues. This tremendous handworking of the surface is something of the opposite of an excavation. Whereas an archaeologist unearths to reveal the complexities of another culture, Robillard's additive process laminates image over image— sometimes as many as ten or more layers—to coalesce a visual sensation of another time and place while simultaneously establishing the images as relics of the present.

> *Cosmos is where the human subject disappears. It is nature, but not the kind of nature that obeys the modern-capitalist registers of cultivation, exploitation, and contemplation.*
>
> Lars Bang Larsen, writing about the artwork
> of Katie Paterson[4]

Robillard's next major body of work, *Luminous Frontiers* (2007), took the artist from the relative intimacy of the city to the macrocosm of deep space. Many modern and contemporary artists have imagined the cosmos, from Wassily Kandinsky to Lucien Rudaux, Vija Celmins, Nancy Graves, Dorothea Rockburne, and conceptual artist Katie Paterson. Robillard's interpretations are firmly within the pictorial tradition of landscape. But Robillard is also deeply engaged by science; at one time, she was an active member of YLEM: Artists Using Science and Technology. Her inquisitiveness led to an investigation of photographs of the celestial bodies captured by the Hubble telescope. Launched in 1990 from the space shuttle *Discovery*, Hubble continues to transmit images of planets, stars, nebulae, and distant galaxies millions of light-years from Earth—a "frontier" that seems as distant now as the West must have seemed to early

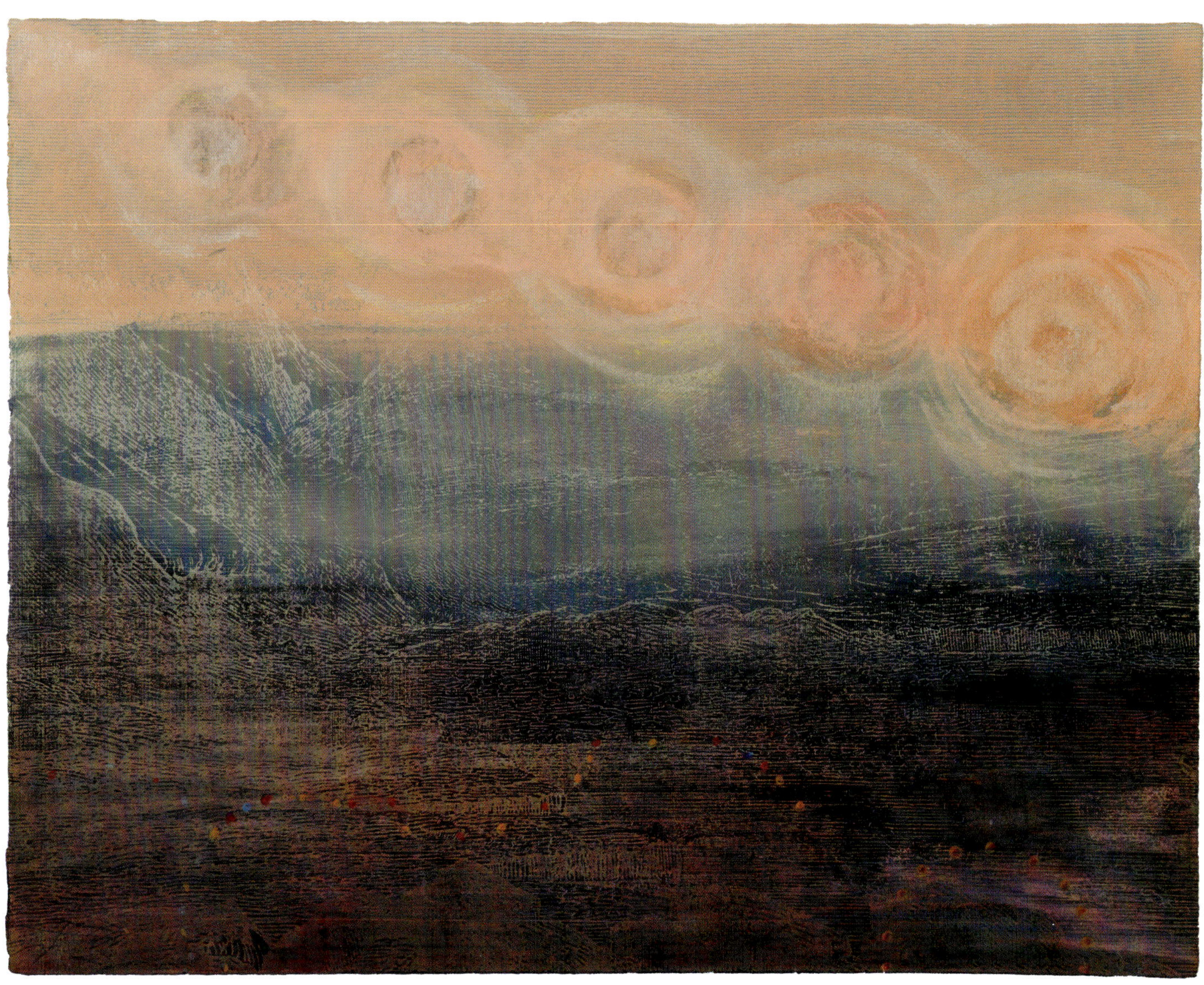

pioneers. If one googles "Hubble telescope," the captivating and otherworldly images that result look like ethereal landscapes. These magnificent images inspired Robillard to conflate visions of the western frontier, again using appropriated nineteenth-century engravings, with overlaid drawings of faraway horizons, mountain ranges, and lush vegetation. Painted onto these distant vistas, Robillard added in whirling orbs, pinwheels, discs, and amoeba-like formations that reference the Hubble-captured gaseous clouds, whorled galaxies, and star clusters—or are they instead symbolic of microbes in the also otherworldly universe seen under a microscope? Works such as *Dove in Space* (fig. 43), *Perpetual Expansion* (fig. 44), or *Space Dance* (fig. 45), confound the viewer by coalescing background, middle ground, and foreground imagery in suggestion of cloud forms, abundant foliage, planetary bodies, and blossom-like forms. Robillard even interjects swirls and spirals—a bit reminiscent of the charged atmosphere of Van Gogh's *Starry Night*—as if to visualize the very energy within the atmosphere of the drawing.[5]

> *For me, trees have always been the most penetrating preachers. I revere them when they live in tribes and families, in forests and groves. And even more I revere them*

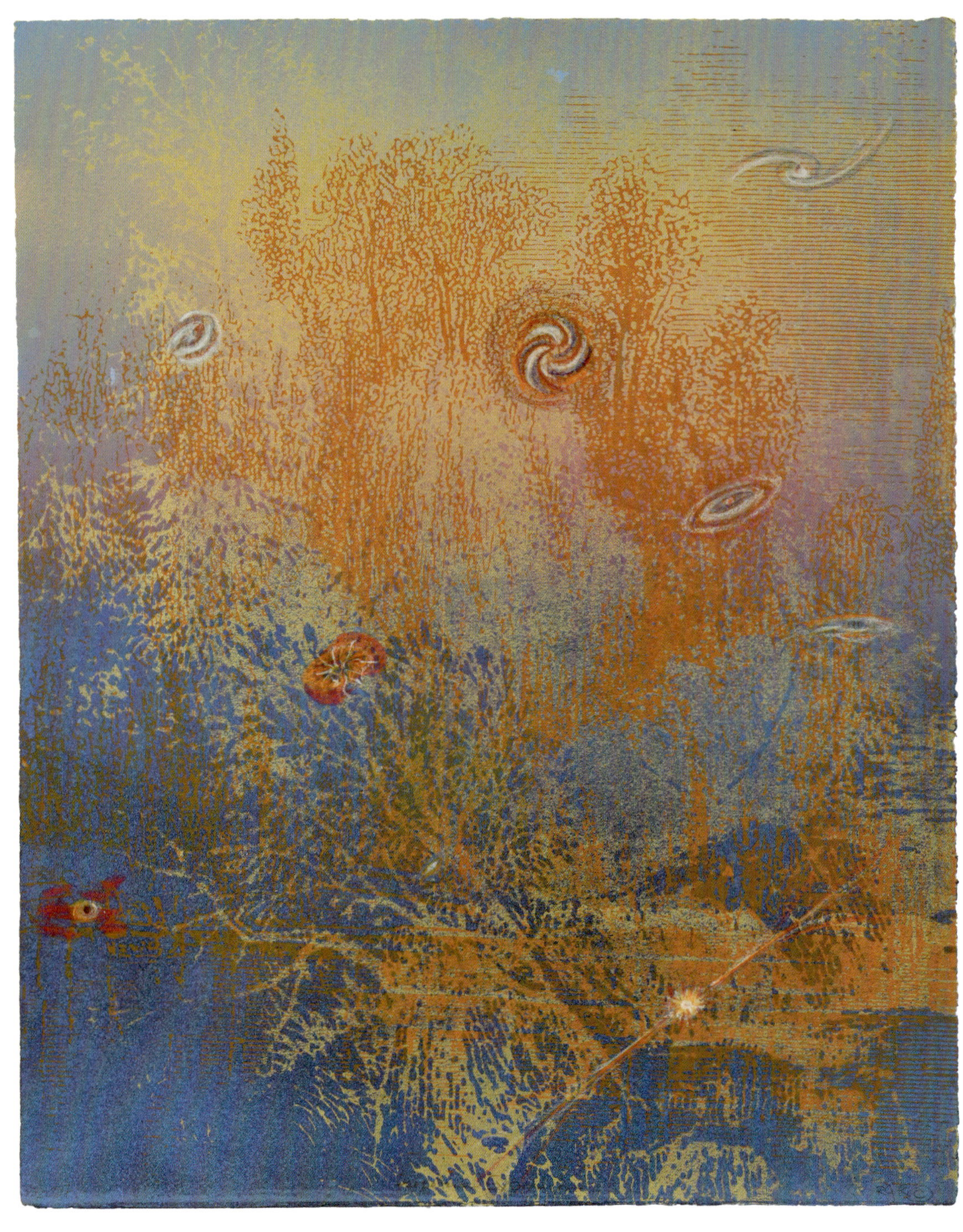

Fig. 44: *Perpetual Expansion*, from the series *Luminous Frontiers*, 2007, screenprint and colored pencil on paper, 22¼ × 18¼ inches, collection of the artist.

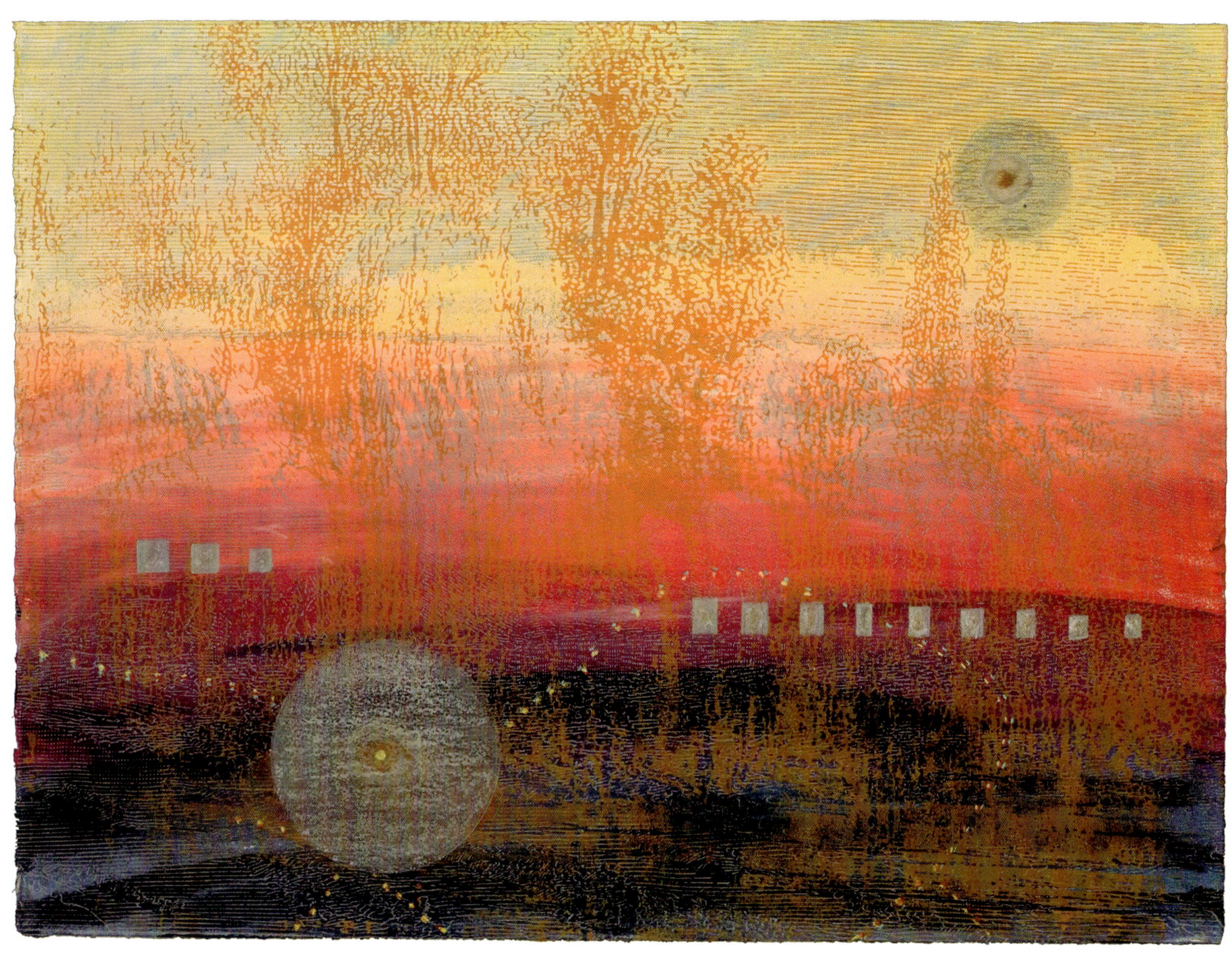

Fig. 45: *Space Dance*, from the series *Luminous Frontiers*, 2007, screenprint and colored pencil on paper, 16¼ × 22¼ inches, Gift of the Artist. Portland Art Museum, Portland, Oregon, © Rita Robillard, 2015.79.5.

when they stand alone. . . . Nothing is holier, nothing is more exemplary than a beautiful, strong tree.

Hermann Hesse[6]

In 2007, Robillard joined a Portland Institute for Contemporary Art trip to China. This was an important opportunity for her, as her own art history background instilled a love for Asian art. During her years living in Berkeley and studying at the University of California, she concentrated on Asian art history and studied under James Cahill, the eminent expert on Chinese art. She was also introduced to the spectacular and comprehensive Avery Brundage Collection (now the Asian Art Museum) in San Francisco. This inculcated a deep respect and resonance with the Asian art aesthetic.

In 2013, Robillard was awarded a residency at the Sitka Center for Art and Ecology in Otis, Oregon. In a typical expression of her interest in intersecting and overlapping disciplines, she worked with scientists studying the Cascade Head Experimental Forest, a swath of land set aside by the Forest Service in 1934 for the study of the coastal rain-forest ecosystem. This very special forest, a Biosphere Reserve, was designated part of UNESCO's Man and the Biosphere program in 1980. Robillard studied the natural evolution of this unique ecological environment, how nature characteristically layers the interconnected life cycles of plants, from mycelium to seeds through decay, to support the health of the entire botanical community. Robillard equates this innate process to the complex and intertwined nature of human history.

This body of work represents a return to a beloved subject—trees—that has occupied Robillard's imagination throughout her career. Her first works based on trees began during a stay at Dorland Mountain Arts Colony in Temecula, California, a two-month residency awarded on Nature Conservancy land. These were followed by her major series of scroll paintings, *Cottonwoods of the Palouse*, from 1993–95 (figs. 6, 36). "My work is a lyrical historiography that uses the landscape as a way of describing who we are, whether it documents where we have been or indicates sublime states of aspiration. I am not alone in determining that we are best described by our surroundings," Robillard says.

At the Sitka residency, Robillard resumed this theme by painting "portraits" of the enormous coniferous trees found in the Coast Range, the mix of Douglas fir, western hemlock, and Sitka spruce. Robillard's monumental *Coastal Range* (2012) is a six-panel, seven-foot-wide painting of a stand of evergreens and deciduous trees massed in a group—or "family" or "tribe"—as they are experienced in a healthy forest (fig. 16). But each tree in this painting is simultaneously individuated and unique. The trees are set against what seems like a gold field; here Robillard was influenced by her roots in Asian art history and her love of Chinese and Japanese screens and scroll paintings. In fact, what appears to be gold leaf is, again, a

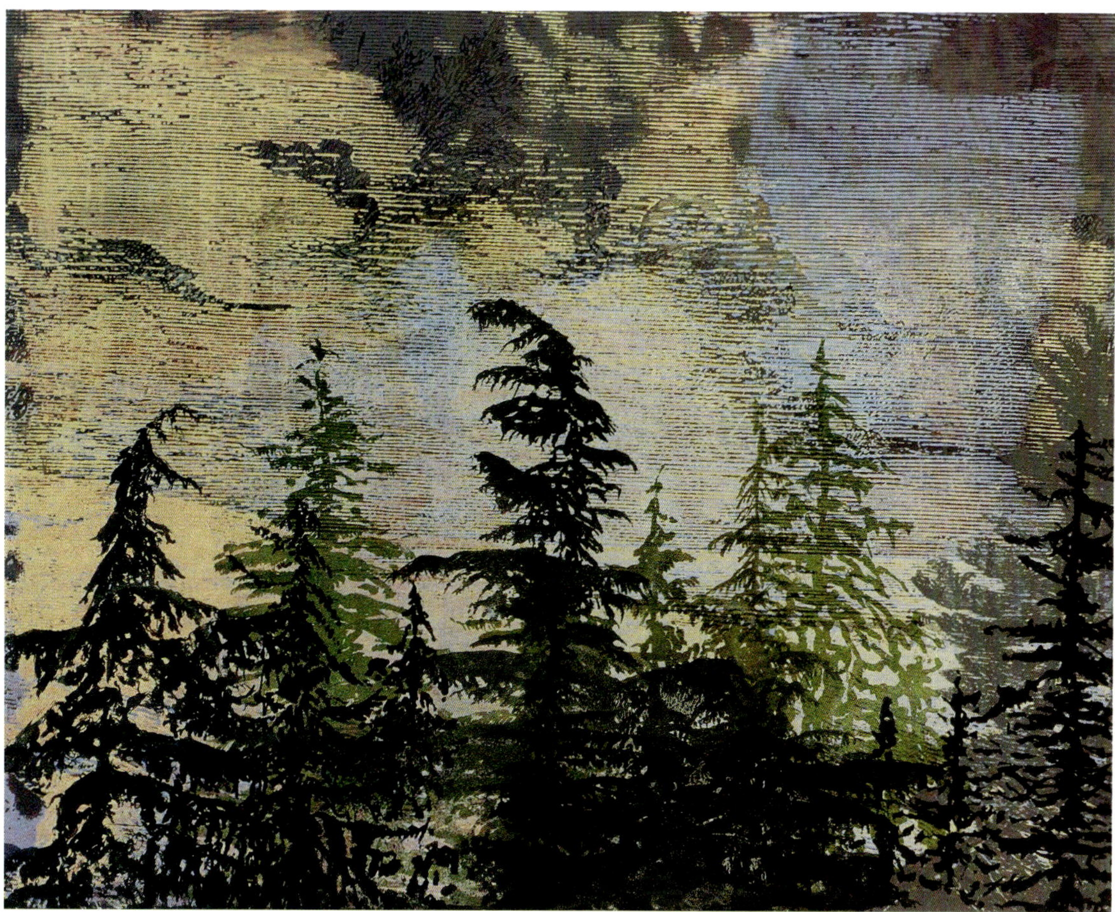

bottom layer of appropriated imagery from vintage etchings, silkscreened onto the panels
and then overpainted. Thus began a series Robillard pursued of innumerable tree paintings,
sometimes depicting a single evergreen and at other times small groups or gatherings of
trees (figs. 46, 47). This trope provided Robillard the opportunity to explore variations in
palette and composition.

> *In fact, artists have their biggest social impact when they achieve it obliquely. . . .*
> *You change the world by changing peoples' hearts and imaginations.*
>
> David Brooks[7]

In 2016, Robillard turned her attention to a series loosely based on issues around climate
change. She called this series *Polarities: Patterns in Time: 1880/2016, 2.3 Degrees Fahrenheit.*[8]
Much of Robillard's immediate source material for this series came from her personal
collection of nineteenth-century travel adventures, especially an 1874 book called *The Polar and
Tropical Worlds: A Description of Man and Nature* by Dr. G. Hartwig.[9] The book itself is about
opposites; it is divided into two sections, one on the icy regions of the Arctic and Antarctic,
the other on the tropical world. Themes include geological, biological, and botanical
observations as well as anthropological accounts of how human beings live in these regions.
Like many familiar nineteenth-century books on natural history, this volume is heavily
illustrated with anonymous engravings having exotic descriptions: "Forms of icebergs," "Chase

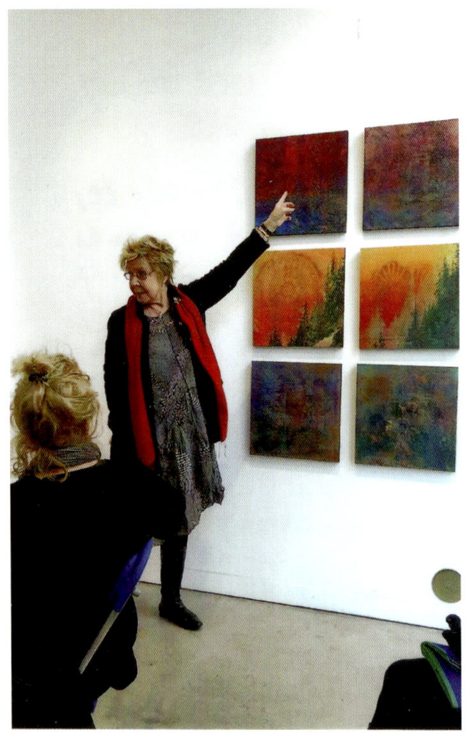

of the walrus," or "Natives of Aru shooting the great bird of paradise." These engravings provided the evocative background imagery for Robillard's *Polarities*.

Reclamation (2016) is a major painted screenprint from this series; here Robillard has once again adopted the format and orientation of a Japanese screen (fig. 48). The six panels depict a verdant equatorial landscape, so atmospheric that the warmth and humidity are nearly palpable. Again, Robillard's study of Asian art history comes into play; she deeply respects the way Asian art often elevates the quotidian into the utterly sublime. There is a sense of theater in this painting, too, and in many others among Robillard's panel paintings, reminding the viewer that the world is a stage, that there is untold drama taking place within the landscape. Robillard says that her use of both Eastern and Western pictorial traditions subtly underscores her belief in the importance of thinking globally.

Incorporated into the layered imagery of *Reclamation* are passages of screened lace, a motif that Robillard has interwoven into all the works in this series.[10] Robillard is indebted to the Pattern and Decoration movement of the 1970s, in which traditionally women's craft-based arts were elevated and celebrated within the canon of "fine art." The gossamer patterns of the lace are in stark contrast to the sweeping landscapes, and they are another allusion to past centuries, parallel to the anonymous nineteenth-century book illustrations. But, equally importantly, this element is one way in which Robillard inserts a sense of the feminine into her work: lacemaking is a domestic art. For Robillard, the use of lace is a hopeful and protective element, a talismanic veil or a wishful shield. The use of antique lace also suggests notions of reclamation—not only the recycling of a doily into a painting but also the larger hope that the earth might be recovered and restored.

The white water lilies that punctuate the pond in the lower band of the painting are also curiously symbolic of male/female duality. After all, it is a male artist, Claude Monet, who is so inextricably associated with painting water lilies, yet Robillard confidently depicts them as her own. In a way, all the works in *Polarities: Patterns in Time* are instances where Robillard has started with the "maleness" of the exploration illustrations and transmuted them into a "female" iteration of the scene. The subtext here is Robillard's faith that all people can participate in the caretaking and nurturance necessary to reclaim the environment.

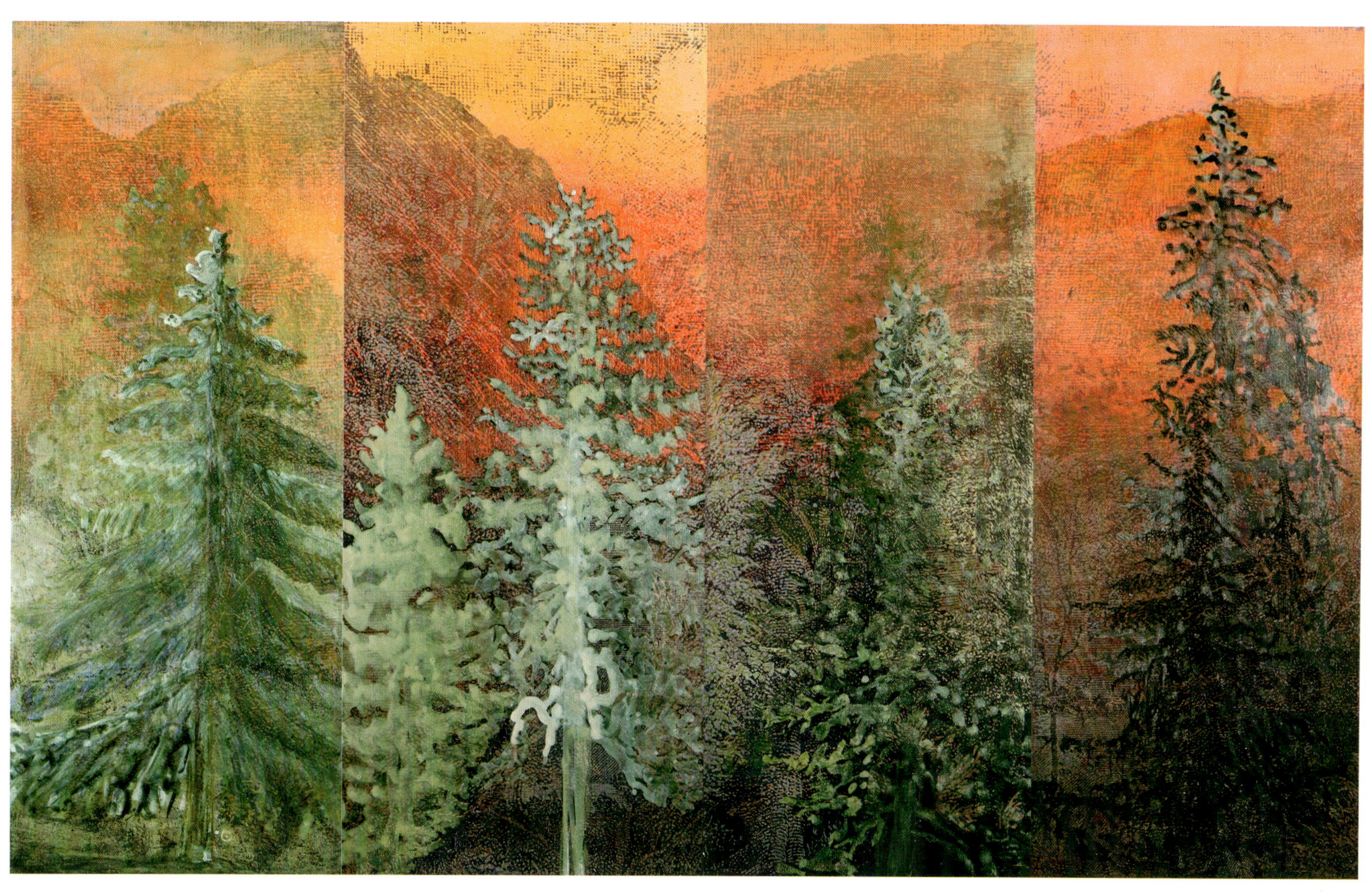

Fig. 47: *Pillars: Trees in the Hills*, from the series *And Then Again: Rifts on the Forest and Time*, 2017, screenprint and acrylic on panel, four prints, 28 × 12 inches each, collection of Freda Sherburne.

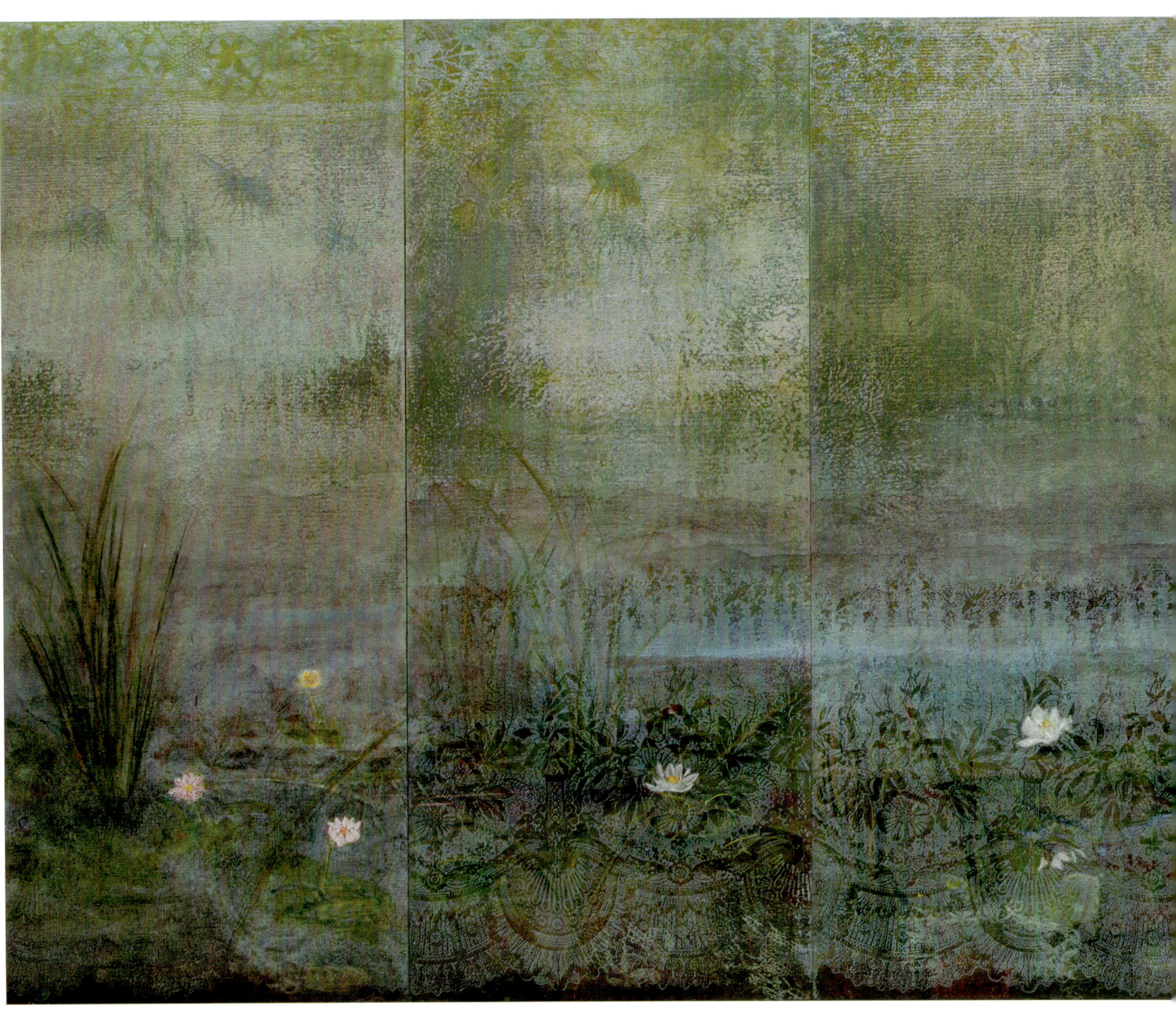

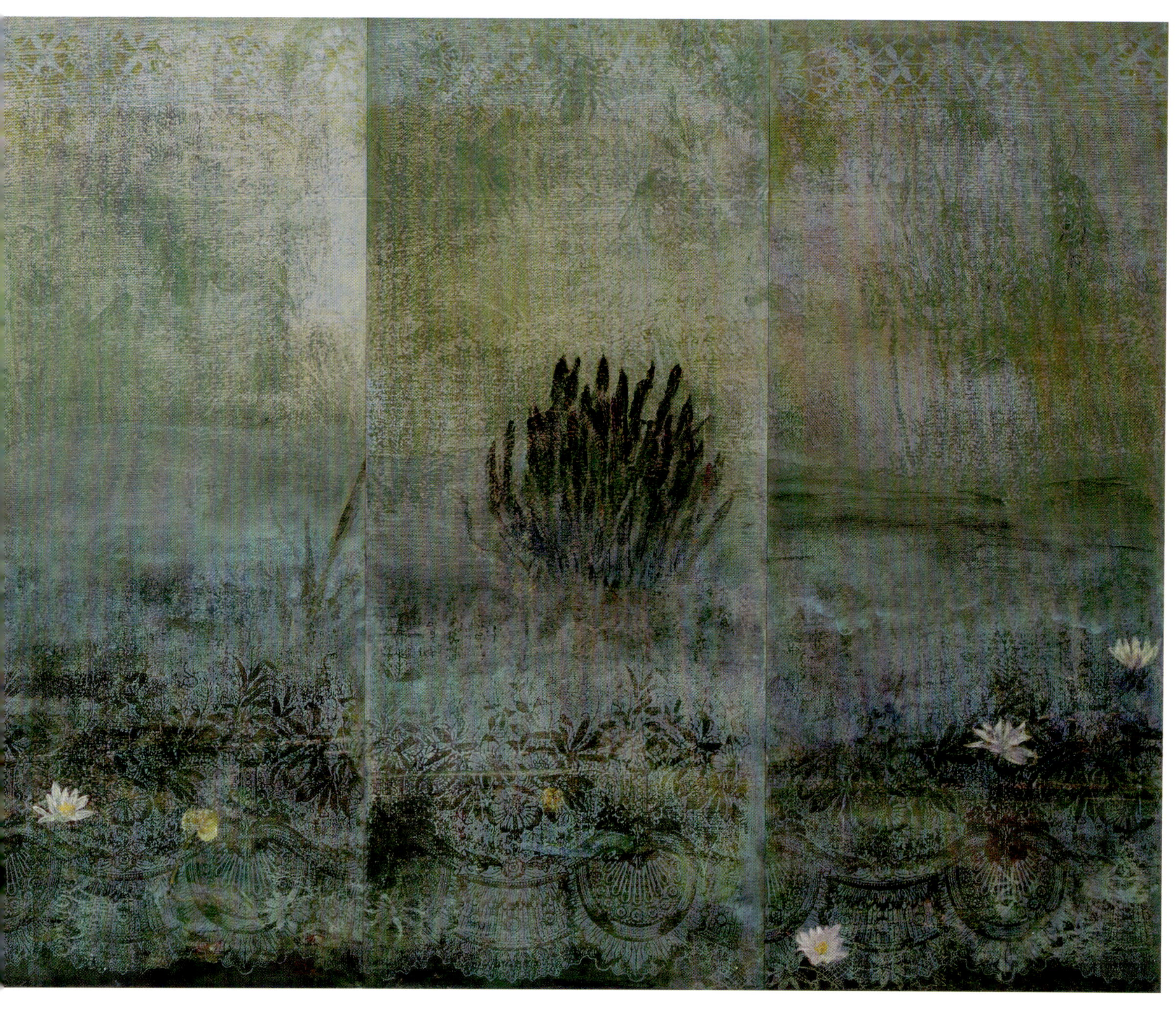

Fig. 48: *Reclamations*,
from the series
*Polarities: Patterns in
Time: 1880/2016, 2.3
Degrees Fahrenheit*, 2016,
screenprint and acrylic
on panel, 27 × 72 inches,
collection of Ross Jory.

In another work in this series, *Deluge* (2016), the central image is an Arctic Ocean scene, frigid and stormy, with glaciers calving into rising waters (fig. 49). Here the blue-black of the ground, the turquoise of the water, and the iridescent silver pigment that traces the landforms convey the extreme cold of this frozen world. So effective is the image that there is the sensation that the ice is melting off the bottom edge of the page. Underneath, ghost images of antique lace—almost like snowflakes—remind the viewer that humankind has had a hand in dramatic climate reversal.

Robillard is acutely aware of the imminent peril that threatens virtually all environments in the twenty-first century, but she resolutely refuses to be dystopic in her vision. She has lived long enough to have witnessed a certain resilience of history—nuclear annihilation has been averted (so far); some species have successfully returned from the brink of extinction— and she is cautiously optimistic. Unlike other contemporary artists who have focused on the Anthropocene, Robillard makes a deliberate decision to depict a world of beauty. She comments that it is hard for her to imagine how images of horror could motivate real change, and it is her choice to revel in the elegant forms and lush colors that typify her work.

> *And here we are, midway through 2020, a year dominated by a global pandemic and the US government's disastrous and deadly response to it, combined with civil unrest the likes of which many of us born in the wake of the 1960s have never seen. . . . In the space of all of this heterogeneous virtuosity, what continually moves me is the human desire to go out and pluck them [flowers] from the earth, to join them into a bouquet, and to arrange them in a container. Why am I still putting flowers in vases during a global pandemic? Why am I still looking at paintings of flowers during a period of massive social upheaval? When is a desire so prevalent that it signifies a need?*
>
> Helen Molesworth[11]

As was the case for many artists during the most intense two years of the COVID-19 pandemic, Robillard found herself alone in her studio and isolated from her community. As a soothing exercise, Robillard turned to a stack of stretched canvases she already had in her studio and started to paint flowers. Unable to silkscreen onto canvas, she employed a lower-tech spray-paint process to stencil layers of lace onto the canvas as ground for compositions involving bouquets of blossoms. This was not an entirely new direction; in Pullman, Robillard had peonies in her garden and would draw them for herself. But during the pandemic, this simple exercise allowed Robillard to surround herself with beauty and enjoy experimenting with compositions and color combinations. Engaging with the comfort of the botanical world is not exactly unique during times of such confusion and sadness—Karma Gallery in the East Village of New York mounted an extraordinarily ambitious exhibition called *(Nothing But) Flowers* in 2020 in which many of the objects in the exhibition were dated to that very year.

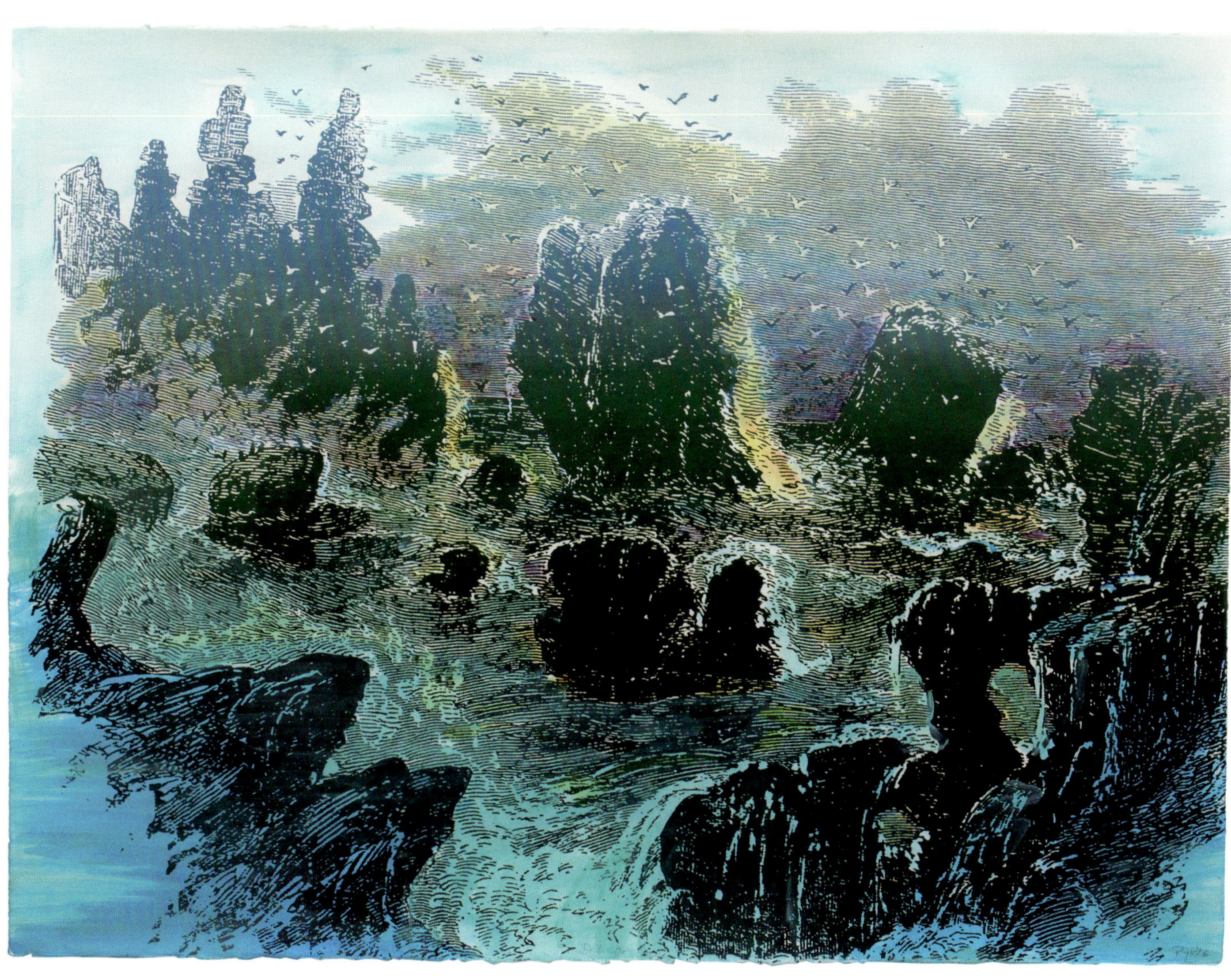

Fig. 49: *Deluge*, from the
series *Polarities: Patterns
in Time: 1880/2016, 2.3
Degrees Fahrenheit*, 2016,
screenprint on paper,
22 × 30 inches, collection
of the Hallie Ford
Museum of Art,
Willamette University,
Salem, Oregon, gift of
the artist, 2018.014.

But the subject matter was a bit of a departure for Robillard. Nonetheless, many of her recent flower paintings include background vintage imagery of Amazon jungle specimens against local flowers from the farmers' market, a subtle acknowledgment that the rain forests of Brazil, dear to Robillard because of her time living in South America, are in jeopardy (fig. 50). With these flower paintings, Robillard comes full circle by conflating global themes—the jungle—with her personal experience of weathering the pandemic in her own studio.

The year 2020 included another project that circled Robillard back to earlier studio work. Under the enforced circumstances of sheltering in place, the choral group In Mulieribus (Latin for "amongst women") shifted their annual concert season to a virtual platform. Under the artistic directorship of Anna Song, the group collaborated with printmakers, photographers, filmmakers, animators, and poets to create integrated multisensory experiences called "Visions in Sound." Robillard was asked to work with the group to use images of her artwork to illustrate the group's concert "Visions of Eternity."[12] Details from Robillard's oeuvre were paired with a song cycle by Andrea Reinkemeyer and text by poet Henrietta Cordelia Ray. Born of the constraints of the pandemic, when audiences could not gather to experience music live, this collaboration with In Mulieribus offered new viewers the opportunity to experience Robillard's work in a fresh way.

Robillard's contemplation of time and place, with its historical underpinnings, is an ongoing inquiry in her work. As an artist and an observer, Robillard is an intrepid seeker in her quest for discovering the world from as many divergent vantage points as possible. Her process—interweaving of histories, overlaying images, and summoning forth a certain beauty—coalesces in the visual poetry of her art.

Linda Tesner is an independent curator and fine arts consultant in Portland, Oregon. She is the former director of the Jordan Schnitzer Museum of Art at Portland State University and the Ronna and Eric Hoffman Gallery of Contemporary Art at Lewis and Clark College in Portland, assistant director of the Portland Art Museum, and director of the Maryhill Museum of Art in Goldendale, Washington. She is the author of numerous exhibition catalogs and monographs and has a special interest in contemporary art.

Notes

1   T. S. Eliot, "Little Gidding," in *Four Quartets* (New York: Ecco Press, 1968).

2   Robillard's painting *Pass* (2001) is a companion painting to *Nch'i-Wána (Columbia River), 1860–2021* (2021). The subject of *Pass* is the mountainous landscape in the Coast Range, the passage from Portland to the Oregon Coast.

3   Robillard credits the following for guiding her around Portland in her research for *Time and Place*: Lois Allan, Eloise Damrosch, Kristy Edmunds, Barbara Fergusson, Susan Fillin-Yeh, Michael Gold, Bruce Guenther, Harvey Hood, Terri Hopkins, Harold Johnson, Chet Orloff, Linda Wysong, and Jen Yeh.

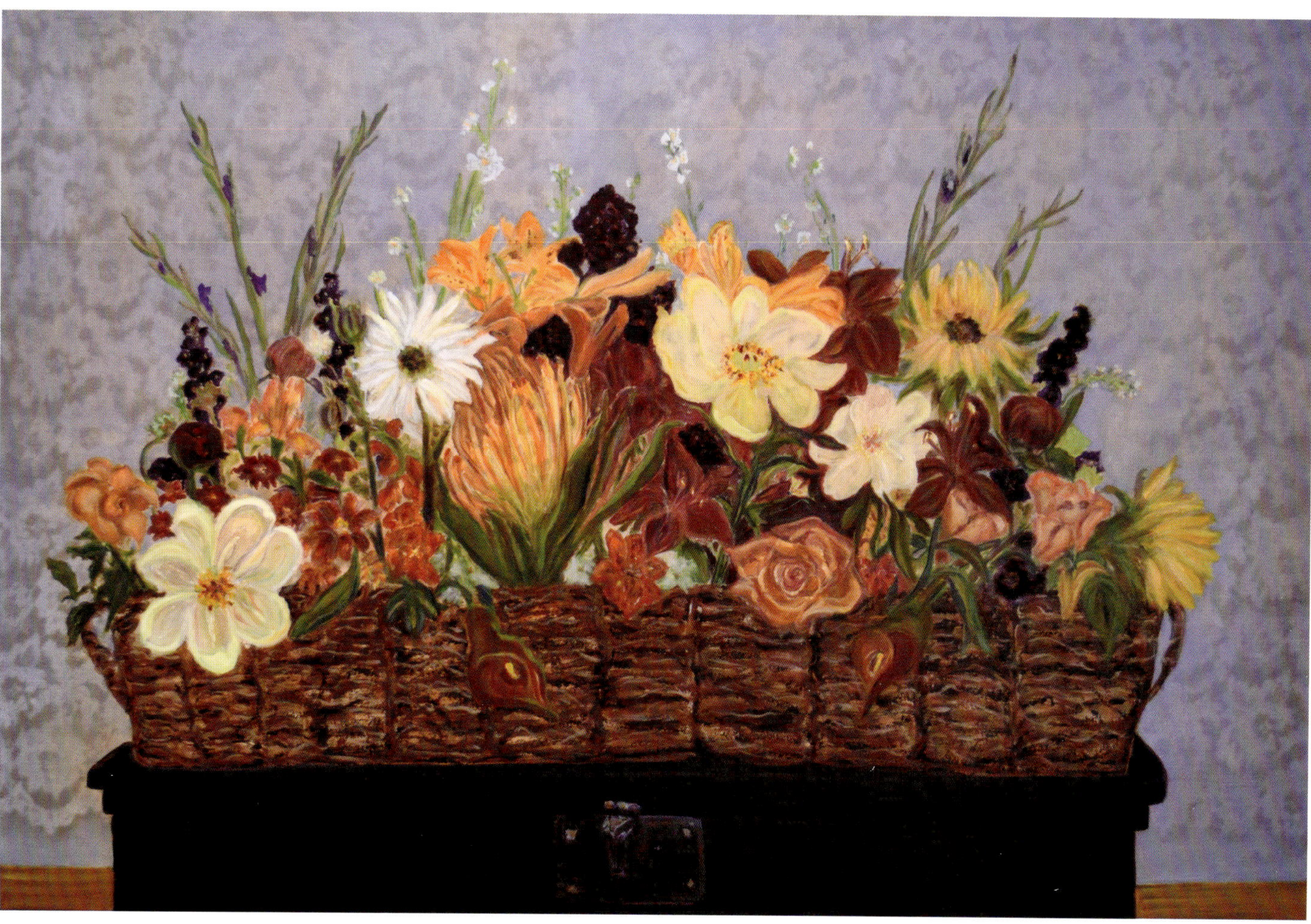

Fig. 50: *Grace*, from the series *Flower Serenade: A Gift of Time*, 2020–21, oil on canvas, 36 × 54 inches, courtesy of the artist and the Augen Gallery.

4   Lars Bang Larsen, "Astronomy Domine: The Anthropological-Cosmological Squeeze in Katie Paterson's Work," Future Library, 2016 (https://www.futurelibrary.no/assets/press/essays/Lars_Bang_Larsen.pdf).

5   For an elegant essay on *The Luminous Frontier*, see Sue Taylor, "Rita Robillard's Poetical Cosmology," in *Place in Time: Contemporary Landscape* (Claremont, California: Scripps College, 2008), 49–54.

6   Hermann Hesse, *Trees: An Anthology of Writings and Paintings* (San Diego, California: Kales Press, 2022), 1.

7   David Brooks, "When Beauty Strikes," *New York Times*, January 15, 2016, https://www.nytimes.com/2016/01/15/opinion/when-beauty-strikes.html.

8   The 2.3 degrees Fahrenheit of the title refers to the increase in average temperature during the first six months of 2016 over the average temperature for the same period in 1880, when global record-keeping began. Henry Fountain, "Global Temperatures Are on Course for Another Record This Year," *New York Times*, July 19, 2016, https://www.nytimes.com/2016/07/20/science/nasa-global-temperatures-2016.html.

9   In the book *The Polar and Tropical Worlds: A Description of Man and Nature*, the illustrations are attributed simply to "designs furnished by artists in the regions to which they relate."

10   Robillard dedicated the series *Polarities: Patterns in Time* to her friend and mentor, the artist Miriam Schapiro (1923–2015), who often used reclaimed lace in her work.

11   Helen Molesworth, "Flowers and Vases," in *(Nothing but) Flowers* (New York: Karma Books, 2021), 16–17.

12   See https://www.inmulieribus.org/.

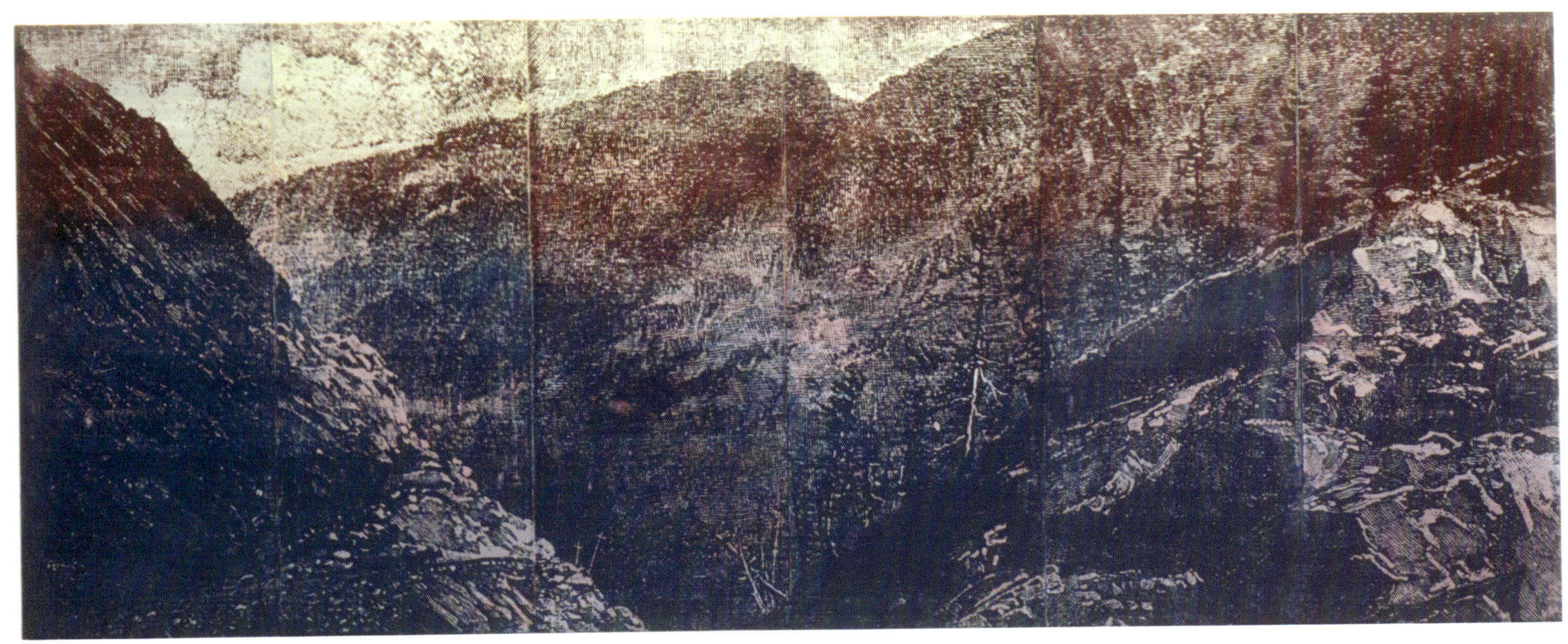

Biography

Born 1944, New York City

Selected Solo Exhibitions

2023

Rita Robillard: Time and Place, Hallie Ford Museum of Art, Willamette University, Salem,
Oregon; curated by John Olbrantz

2021

Flower Serenade: A Gift of Time, Augen Gallery, Portland, Oregon

2020

Votives & Polarities, Dengerink Gallery, Washington State University, Vancouver, Washington

2019

The Waters of March—Spring, Augen Gallery, Portland, Oregon

2016

Polarities: Patterns in Time, 1880/2016, 2.3 Degrees Fahrenheit, Augen Gallery, Portland, Oregon
Here & Then: Timeless Migrations, Kittredge Gallery, University of Puget Sound, Tacoma,
Washington

2014

Renewing Time, Caressing the Moment, Augen Gallery, Portland, Oregon

2013

And Then Again: Rifts on the Forest and Time, Augen Gallery, Portland, Oregon

2009

Lookout/Outlook, Littman Gallery, Smith Center, Portland State University, Portland, Oregon
Lookout/Outlook, video shown at Fulcrum Gallery, New York City

2006

The Oregon Breast Center, Beaverton, Oregon

2004

Arranging Experiences, Glenn & Viola Walters Cultural Arts Center, Hillsboro, Oregon

The Pass, from the series
Time and Place, 2001,
screenprint and acrylic
on panel, 28 × 72 inches,
courtesy of the artist and
the Augen Gallery.

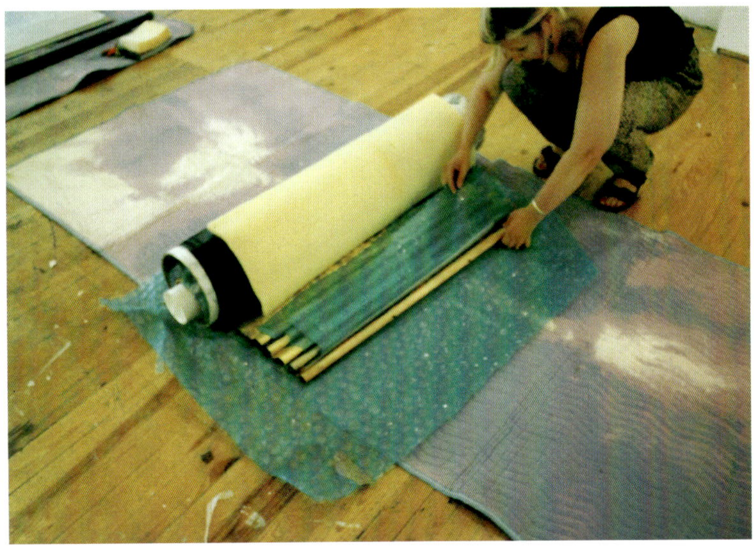

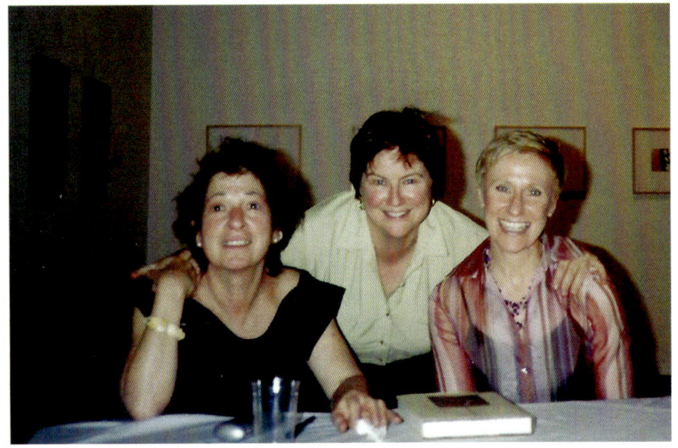

2003

Wandering, Lorinda Knight Gallery, Spokane, Washington

2002

Governor's Office, State Capitol, Salem, Oregon

Coming West to Meet the East, Dean's Office, Washington State University, Vancouver,
    Washington

2001

Time and Place, Elizabeth Leach Gallery, Portland, Oregon

1998

Essence and Artifice: Views of Spokane, Lorinda Knight Gallery, Spokane, Washington

1997

The Garden, the Park, and the Fall from Grace, A.I.R. Gallery, New York City

1991

Windows, Gallery II, Fine Art Center, Washington State University, Pullman, Washington

1990

Windows, Wentz Gallery, Pacific Northwest College of Art, Portland, Oregon

1987

Spirit Ground, Ruth Chandler Williamson Gallery, Scripps College, Claremont, California

Left: Rita installing *Cottonwoods of the Palouse* scrolls at the A.I.R. Gallery, New York City, 1997.

Right: A panel discussion at the Elizabeth Leach Gallery in Portland, Oregon, with, from left to right, Susan Fillen-Yeh, Elizabeth Leach, and Sue Taylor, 2001.

Selected Group Exhibitions

2019

Forest Visions, Royal Nebeker Gallery, Clatsop College, Astoria, Oregon; curated by Bonnie
    Laing-Malcolmson

2018

Landscapes, Augen Gallery, Portland, Oregon

2016

From the Collection: New Acquisitions, Jordan Schnitzer Museum of Art, Washington State
    University, Pullman, Washington
Nature as Metaphor, Augen Gallery, Portland, Oregon

2015

Prints and Drawings Spanning 500 Years, Portland Art Museum, Portland, Oregon
Augen Gallery, Portland, Oregon

2014

Women and Print: A Contemporary View, Ruth Chandler Williamson Gallery, Scripps College,
    Claremont, California

2012

Sitka Art Invitational, World Forestry Center, Portland, Oregon
Kala Art Institute, Berkeley, California

2010

Augen Gallery, Portland, Oregon

2008

Place and Time: Contemporary Landscape, Ruth Chandler Williamson Gallery, Scripps College,
    Claremont, California

2007

Art in Embassies Program, US State Department, Port Moresby, Papua New Guinea

2005

Eco Trust, Portland, Oregon

2004

Biosphere, The Arts Center, Saratoga Springs, New York
Dialogue: A Faculty and Student Exhibition, University of Ulsan, South Korea, and Portland
    State University, Portland, Oregon
The Gorge Park, Lorinda Knight Gallery, Spokane, Washington

2003

The Journey's End, Columbia River Maritime Museum, Astoria, Oregon
Print Arts Northwest, Portland, Oregon

2002

Facing Faces, Hyundai Art Gallery, Ulsan, South Korea

2000

Elizabeth Leach Gallery, Portland, Oregon

Disintegration: Contemporary Landscape, Elizabeth Leach Gallery, Portland, Oregon

Open Walls, Portland Institute for Contemporary Art, Portland, Oregon

The 21st Century: New Paradigm, Mugeo Gallery, University of Ulsan, South Korea; traveled to Kyushu Sangyo University, Fukuoka, Japan, and Portland State University, Portland, Oregon

1999

Art in Embassies Program, US State Department, Yaoundé, Cameroon

Print Invitational, Coburn Art Gallery, Ashland University, Ashland, Ohio

Cairns, Quilts, Contact, Ink People Gallery, Eureka, California

Vancouver School of Arts and Academics, Vancouver, Washington

1998

Prints Across the Pacific, China National Academy of Fine Art, Hongzhou; curated by Gordon Gilkey and Susan Fillin-Yeh

Governor's Office, State Capitol, Olympia, Washington

Works on Paper, New York Armory, hosted by Samson Fine Art, New York City

Local Press, Kittredge Gallery, University of Puget Sound, Tacoma, Washington

1997

Summer Solstice, Lorinda Knight Gallery, Spokane, Washington

Willard Gallery, Kansas State University, Manhattan, Kansas

Northwest Print Council Gallery, Portland, Oregon

Histories and Legacies, Worth Ryder Gallery, University of California, Berkeley, California

1996

Northwest Visions, USIS Serviço de Divulagação and Relações Culturais dos EUA, São Paulo, Brazil; traveled to Fundाção Cultural de Curitiba Museu da Gravura, Curitiba, Brazil

1995

Art Concepts, Walnut Creek Civic Center Gallery, Walnut Creek, California

Contemporary Prints, National '95, Clara M. Lovett Art Museum, Northern Arizona University, Flagstaff, Arizona; curated by Richard Beasley

Land, Tacoma Art Museum, Washington; juried by Jaune Quick-to-See Smith

19th Harper National Print & Drawing Exhibition, Harper College, Pallatine, Illinois; juried by James Yood

Latent August, NJAHS, Pier 1, Fort Mason Center, San Francisco, California; juried by Yoshido Kakudo and Karen Tsujimoto

Fallen Timber, Tacoma Art Museum, Washington; curated by Greg Bell

1994

Un Marco por la Tierra: Proyecto de Integración Latinoamericana de Arte y Ecología, Museo de
    Arte Contemporáneo, Universidad de Chile, Santiago, Chile; curated by Ernesto Muñoz
Diversity and Vision of the Printed Image, Triton Museum of Art, Santa Clara, California
Exquisite Drawing: Lines of Correspondence, Transmission Gallery, Glasgow, Scotland

1993

15 from America, Artetage Gallery, Vladivostok, Russia; traveled to Khabarovsk, Russia
Yes, in My Back Yard? A Portrait of the Nuclear Age, Past, Present, Future, Allied Arts Gallery,
    Richland, Washington; curated by Helen Slade
Lacoste School of the Arts, Lacoste, France

1992

Casting Light, Acknowledging the Shadow: A Tribute to Sylvia Lark, Jordan Schnitzer
    Museum of Art (formerly the Museum of Art), Washington State University, Pullman,
    Washington; curated by Barbara Coddington and Rita Robillard
Southern Printmakers '92; juried by Lee Chesney; traveled to University of Alabama,
    Tuscaloosa, Alabama; Montgomery College, Rockville, Maryland; Morehead State
    University, Morehead, Kentucky; Purdue University, West Lafayette, Indiana
Northwest Prints, Fine Arts Gallery, University of Alberta, Edmonton
Contemporary Prints, Columbia Arts Center, Vancouver, Washington
Alumni Exhibition, Cooper Union, New York City
The Apocalyptic Vision, Walters Hall Gallery, Rutgers University, the State University of New
    Jersey, New Brunswick, New Jersey; curated by Judith Brodsky
Relief Prints, Haynes Fine Arts Gallery, Montana State University, Bozeman, Montana
'91 Invitational Monotype Exhibition, Kipp Gallery, Indiana University of Pennsylvania,
    Indiana

1991

Northwest Printmakers in Washington, State Capitol, Olympia, Washington
Exhibition '91, Berkeley Art Center, Berkeley, California; juried by Archana Horsting, Nathan
    Oliveira, and Lawrence Rindler
Northwest Prints, Portland Art Museum, Portland, Oregon; curated by Mary Priester, Vickie
    Halper, and George Johanson; traveled to the University of Hawaii, Honolulu; Boise
    State University, Idaho; and the Visual Arts Center, Anchorage, Alaska

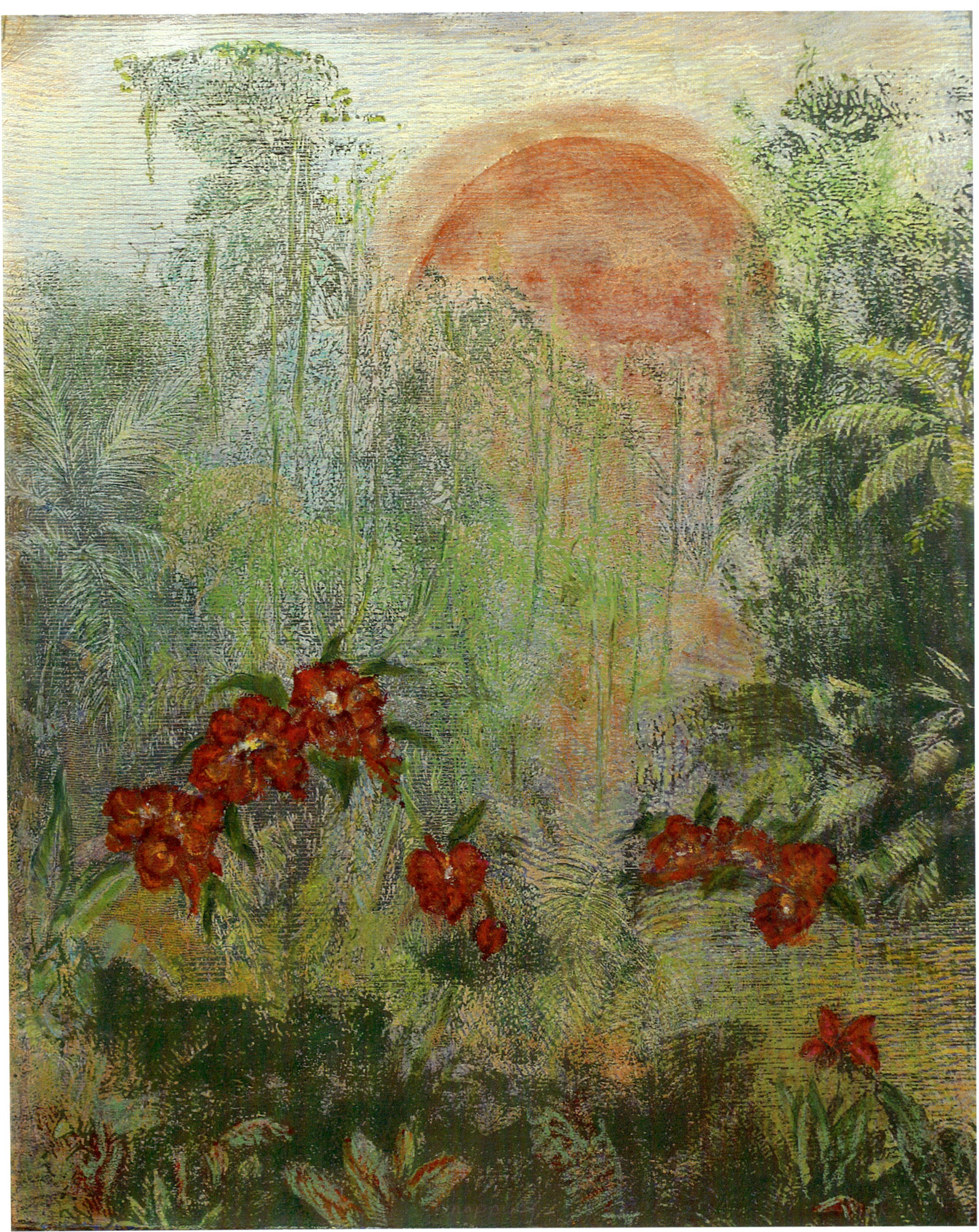

Selected Collections

Banco do Itú, São Paulo, Brazil

Bancroft Library, University of California, Berkeley

Berkeley Art Museum, California

Brooklyn Museum Library, New York

Clorox Corporation, Oakland, California

Consolidated Capital, Emeryville, California

Cooper-Hewitt Museum, New York City

The David Winton Bell Gallery, Brown University, Providence, Rhode Island

Flaxman Library, School of the Art Institute of Chicago, Illinois

Franklin Furnace, New York City

Griswold Museum, Old Lyme, Connecticut

Hallie Ford Museum of Art, Willamette University, Salem, Oregon

Jordan Schnitzer Museum of Art, Washington State University, Pullman, Washington

Kala Art Institute, Berkeley, California

Los Angeles County Museum of Art, California

Massachusetts Institute of Technology Library, Cambridge

Museu da Gravura, Curitiba, Brazil

Museum of Art, Rhode Island School of Design, Providence

Museum of Modern Art Library, New York City

National Academy of Fine Art, Hongzhou, China

Newark Public Library, New Jersey

Newport Art Museum, Rhode Island

New York Public Library, New York City

North Dakota Museum of Art, Grand Forks

Portland Art Museum, Oregon

Ruth Chandler Williamson Gallery, Scripps College, Claremont, California

Smithsonian American Art Museum, Washington, DC

Visual Chronicle of Portland, Regional Arts & Culture Council, Oregon

Whitney Museum of American Art Library, New York City

Yale University Art and Architecture Library, New Haven, Connecticut

Tropical Visions, from the series *Polarities: Patterns in Time: 1880/2016, 2.3 Degrees Fahrenheit*, 2021, screenprint and crayon on paper, 22 × 18½ inches, courtesy of the artist and the Augen Gallery.

Selected Publications

Allan, Lois, Macy Chadwick, Chen Youngi, Eric Dayton, Russ Dodd, Hsingyuan Tsao, Liz Lee, and Kevin Yang. *Prints Across the Pacific*. Hongzhou, China: China National Academy of Fine Art, 1998.

Apgar, Evelyn. "Arts Activity at R.U. Reaches Volcanic Proportions." *Home News* [New Brunswick, New Jersey], July 7, 1991.

Apgar, Evelyn. "Rutgers Exhibit Not for the Squeamish." *Home News* [New Brunswick, New Jersey], July 21, 1991.

"Arte Ecológico en Museo de Arte Contemporáneo." *El Mercurio de Santiago* [Santiago, Chile], September 27, 1994.

Baggio, Antonio M. *Un Marco por la Tierra: Proyecto de Integración Latinoamericana de Arte y Ecología*. Santiago, Chile: Museo de Arte Contemporáneo, Universidad de Chile, 1994.

Bell, Greg. *Fallen Timber*. Tacoma, Washington: Tacoma Art Museum, 1995.

Boas, Pat. "Portland." *Art Papers* magazine, March/April 2002.

Brunson, Jamie. "Nature as Spirituality." *Artweek*, September 20, 1986.

Bryant, Elizabeth. "Fallen Timber." *Artweek*, February 5, 1995.

Cameron, Laura. "The Arts." *Daily Evergreen*, October 7, 1993.

Cohn, Terri. "Conquistadors of the Void." *Artweek*, April 1998.

Dialogue: A Faculty and Student Exhibition. Portland, Oregon: Portland State University, 2004.

Fillin-Yeh, Susan, and Rita Robillard. *Time and Place: Artwork by Rita Robillard*. Portland, Oregon: Elizabeth Leach Gallery, 2001.

Fugitt, Patricia J. *Coastal Currents: A California / New York Exhibition.* Corpus Christi, Texas: Center for the Arts, 1981.

Gillis, Brian, and Kate Wagle, eds. *Connective Conversations: Curator/Critic Tours and Lectures, 2015–2019*. Eugene, Oregon: University of Oregon, 2020.

Haynes, Deborah J. "Centered on the Circumference: Life and Death, Growth and Sex in Eastern Washington." *Visions: Los Angeles Art Quarterly*, March 1992.

Haynes, Deborah J. "The Palouse: Choose to Live Here." *Reflex*, November 1995.

Mathews-Berenson, Margaret. *Women and Print: A Contemporary View*. Claremont, California: Ruth Chandler Williamson Gallery, Scripps College, 2014.

McCarthy, John. "Forest, Fantasy on Tap at Prichard." *Lewiston Tribune*, May 25, 1990.

McCarthy, John. "A View from the Forest." *Lewiston Tribune*, September 1, 1989.

Navarra, Tova. "Six Women Artists Show Their Visions." *Asbury Park Press* [Asbury Park, New Jersey], July 18, 1991.

Raquet, Murf. "Exhibiting Vast Horizons." *Moscow-Pullman Daily News*, October 7, 1991.

Row, D. K. "Beyond the Landscape." *Oregonian*, May 4, 2000.

Shere, Charles. "Two Contrasting Art Shows Find Balance in a Third." *Oakland Tribune*, September 9, 1986.

Slade, Helen. *Yes, in My Back Yard*. Richland, Washington: Allied Arts Gallery, 1993.

Sommer, Waldemar. "En el Museo de Arte Contemporáneo." *La Epoca*, October 23, 1994.

Taylor, Sue. "Rita Robillard at Elizabeth Leach." *Art in America*, May 2002.

Taylor, Sue. "Rita Robillard's Poetic Cosmology," in *Time in Place: Contemporary Landscape*. Claremont, California: Ruth Chandler Williamson Gallery, Scripps Gallery, 2008.

White, Vera. "Prichard Exhibits Show Artists' Mysterious Side." *Idahonian*, June 2–3, 1990.

Awards, Grants, and Residencies

2021
McCanna House, North Dakota Museum of Art, Grand Forks, North Dakota; one month

2012
Residency, Kala Art Institute, Berkeley, California; three months

2011–12
Ford Family Foundation Artist Grant to participate in a residency at the Sitka Center for Art and Ecology, Otis, Oregon; three months

2008
Oregon Arts Commission Career Opportunity Grant

2006
Teaching Excellence Award, Portland State University, Portland, Oregon

2003
The Clark Award, Columbia River Maritime Museum, Astoria, Oregon
Residency, Artist's Enclave at I-Park, East Haddam, Connecticut; two weeks

1996

College Art Association of America (CAA) Mentor Grant, to travel to CAA Conference in
    Boston with graduate student Kyung Kong, who was awarded the 1996 Protégé Grant

1995

Initiation Grant, Washington State University, Pullman, for electronic imaging

1994

Summer School Grant, Washington State University, Pullman, to visit artists' studios for Art
    on Location class in New York City; studio visits included Robert Blackburn and the
    Printmaking Workshop, Shirin Neshat, the Art and Architecture Storefront, and Robert
    Kushner.

1992

Awarded a studio, living quarters, and a stipend for four months to participate in a residency,
    Lacoste, France.

1990

Awarded a two-month residency to draw and complete a series of prints on Nature
    Conservancy land, Dorland Mountain Arts Colony, Temecula, California
Summer Stipend, Washington State University, Pullman

1989

Initiation Grant, Washington State University, Pullman, for photo printmaking
Grant-in-Aid, Washington State University, Pullman, for water-based screenprinting and
    computer application in printmaking

1985

Print Award, California State Fair

Education

1979–81

MFA, University of California, Berkeley

1977–79

BA, University of California, Berkeley, with honors

1962–66

Cooper Union, New York City

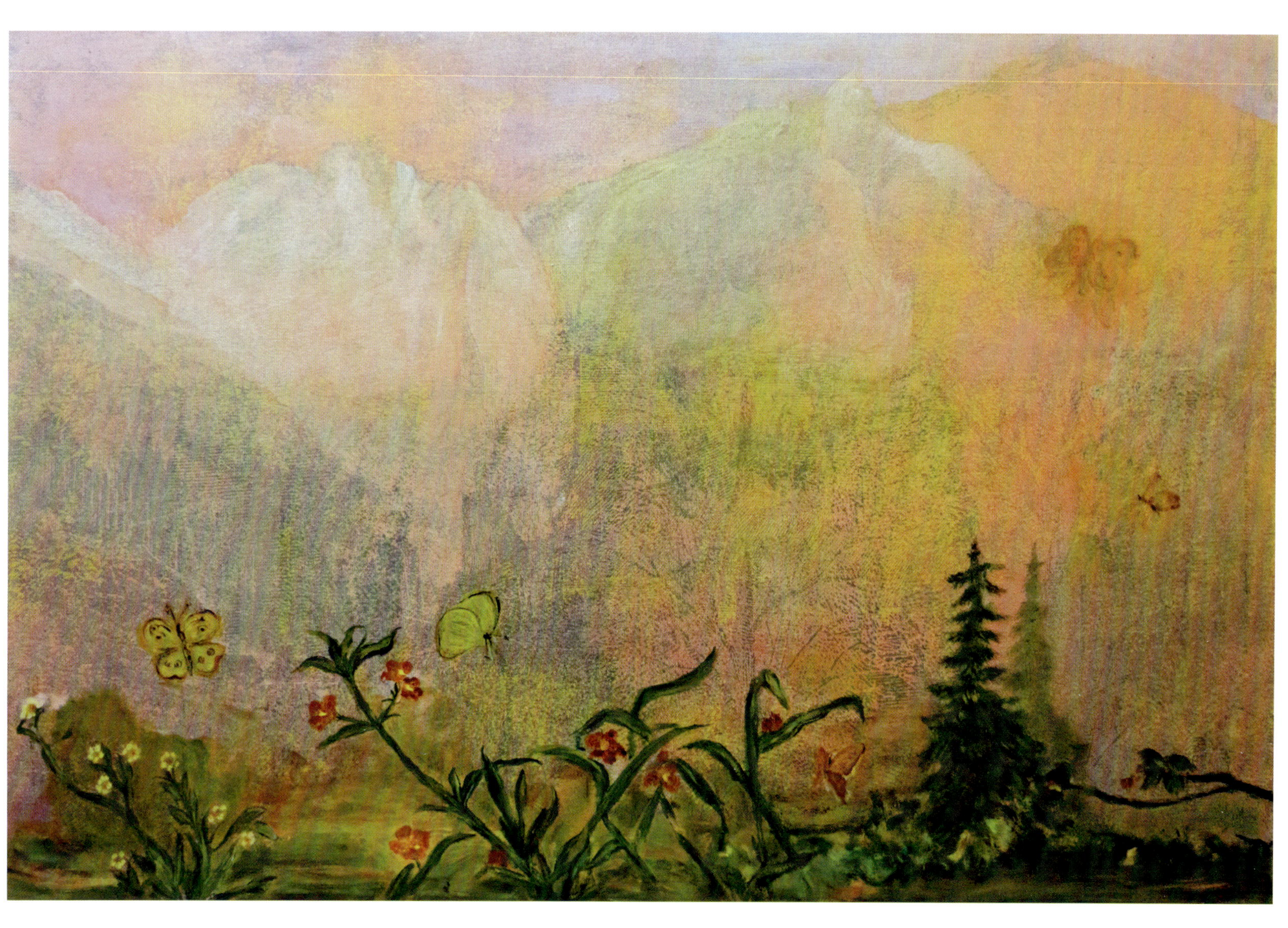

Manifest Destiny Meets Walt, from the series *Flower Serenade: A Gift of Time*, 2022, screenprint and oil on panel, 24 × 36 inches, courtesy of the artist and the Augen Gallery.

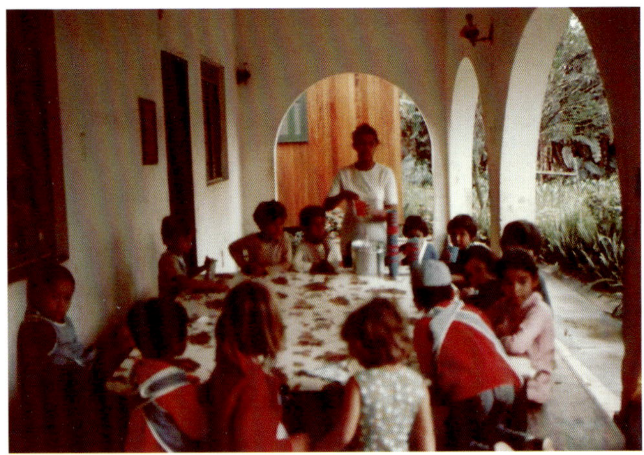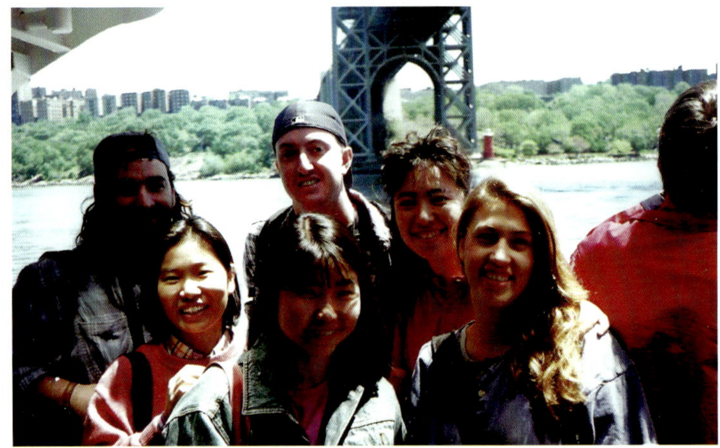

Teaching Experience

1998–2013
Professor, Art Department, Portland State University, Oregon
Taught courses in drawing, mixed media, professional practices, and graduate seminars
Department Chair, 1998–2001; Graduate MFA Chair, 2005–7; Graduate Faculty, 2000–2008;
  Professor Emerita, 2013–present

1993
Visiting Professor, Rhode Island School of Design, Providence, Rhode Island
Taught course in new genre printmaking

1986–98
Assistant to Full Professor, Fine Arts Department, Washington State University, Pullman
Taught courses in figure drawing, printmaking, and graduate seminars
Undergraduate Coordinator and Printmaking Chair, 1986–98; Graduate Faculty, 1987–98

1984–85
Adjunct Instructor, Art Department, Chabot College, Livermore, California
Taught courses in drawing

1982–84
Adjunct Instructor, San Francisco Art Institute, California
Taught courses in photo printmaking

1981
Adjunct Instructor, Art Department, University of California, Davis
Taught courses in figure drawing and photo printmaking

1974
Fundação Alvares Penteado School of Art, São Paulo, Brazil
Taught art to children K–6

Left: Rita teaching an art class in rural Brazil, 1972.

Right: Summer trip with Washington State University students to New York City to visit artist studios, 1994.

Related Experience

2021

Visions of Eternity, an online concert by the In Mulieribus, a female vocal ensemble based in
Portland, Oregon; song cycle by Andrea Reinkemeyer, text by Henrietta Cordelia Ray,
and images by Rita Robillard.

2019

Juror, Sitka residencies, Sitka Center for Art and Ecology, Otis, Oregon

2016

Juror, Percent for Art, Karl Miller Center, Portland State University, Oregon
Co-curator, with Christy Wycoff, *Nature as Memory*, Augen Gallery, Portland, Oregon
Lecture, Kittredge Gallery, University of Puget Sound, Tacoma, Washington

2015

Lecture, Ruth Chandler Williamson Gallery, Scripps College, Claremont, California

2010

Juror, North Bank Gallery, Vancouver, Washington

2008

Panelist, *Place in Time: Contemporary Landscape*, Ruth Chandler Williamson Gallery, Scripps
College, Claremont, California

2007

Juror, Percent for Art, Ondine Residence Hall, Portland State University, Portland, Oregon

2005

Artist in Residence, University of Minnesota, Duluth

2003–8

Board of Directors, Graphics Arts Council, Portland Art Museum, Oregon

2002

Panelist, Arts Industry Development Grant, Oregon Arts Commission

2000

Juror, Visual Arts Fellowship for Individual Artists, Regional Arts and Culture Council,
Portland, Oregon

1998

Lecture, Ruth Chandler Williamson Gallery, Scripps College, Claremont, California
Juror, Corvallis Art Center, Oregon

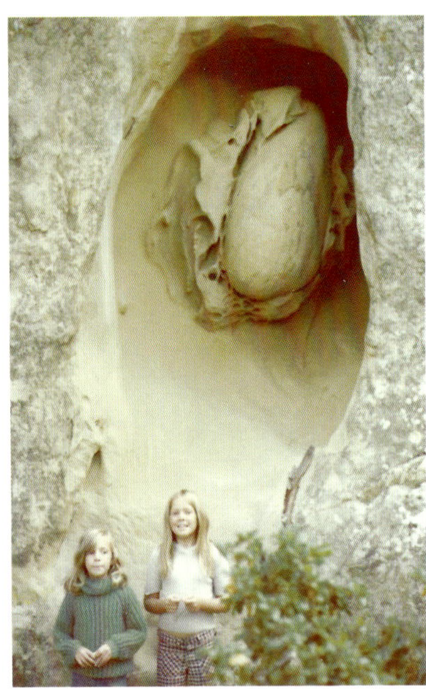

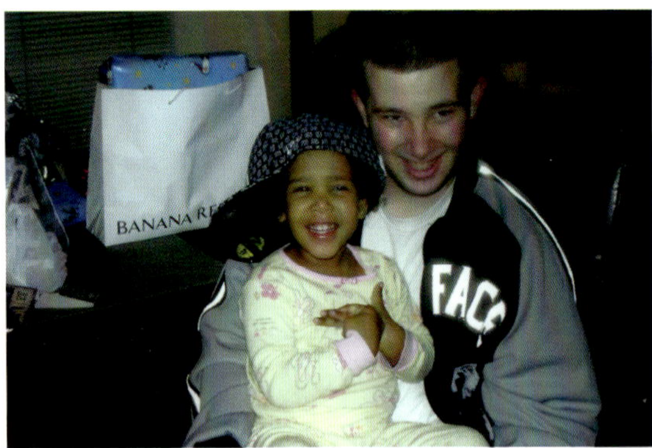

Left: Rita's daughter's Rana (left) and Danielle (right) at Mount Diablo, California, 1974.

Right: Rita's grandchildren Isabella Simone Goines (left) and Cary McNeely (right) at Rana's house in California, 2005.

1995

Panelist, *Collaborative Works in Contemporary Art*, Whitman College, Walla Walla,
    Washington
Visiting Artist, City College of New York

1994–98

Board of Directors, College Art Association
Chair, Publications and Program Committees; Chair, Visual Arts Committee

1992

Visiting Artist, Bradley University, Peoria, Illinois
Co-curator, with Barbara Coddington, *Casting Light, Acknowledging the Shadow: A Tribute
    to Sylvia Lark*, Jordan Schnitzer Museum of Art (formerly the Museum of Art),
    Washington State University, Pullman

1991

Panelist, *Creators or Destroyers: Ethics, the Environment, and Art Materials*, College Art
    Association Annual Meeting, Washington, DC
Visiting Artist, University of Hawaii, Mānoa, Hawaii
Visiting Artist, Pacific Northwest College of Art, Portland, Oregon

1984–85

Editor, *California Printmaker*

1981–83

Board of Directors, California Society of Printmakers

Queen of the Night II, from the series *Flower Serenade: A Gift of Time*, 2021, screenprint and oil on panel, 18 × 18 inches, courtesy of the artist and the Augen Gallery.

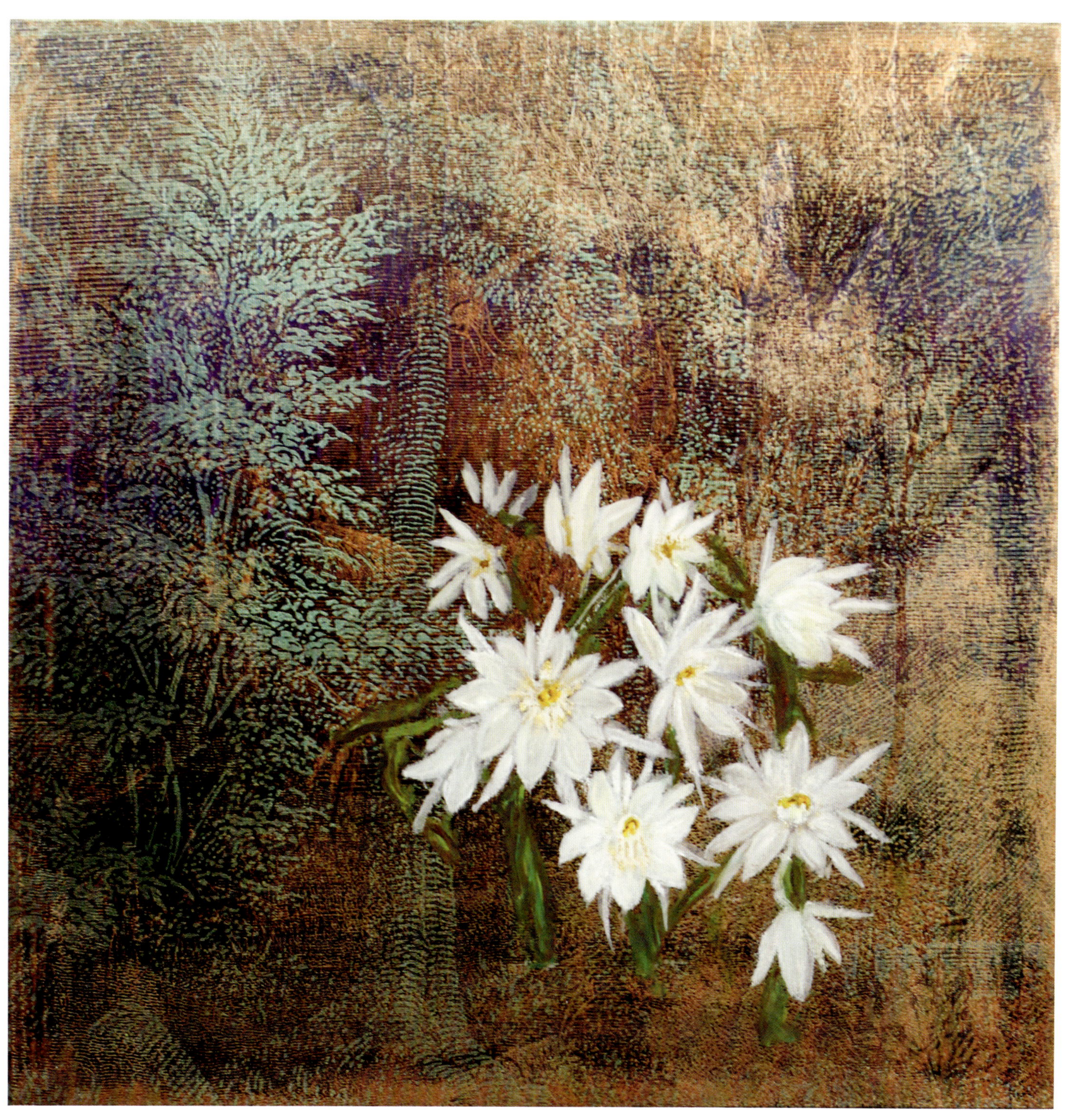

Rita Robillard: Time and Place was organized by the Hallie Ford Museum of Art at Willamette University in Salem, Oregon. The exhibition was held from January 24 to March 25, 2023. Financial support for the exhibition and book was provided by a grant from the Ford Family Foundation; by gifts from several anonymous donors; with funds from the HFMA Exhibition Fund and the Maribeth Collins Art Exhibition Fund; by advertising support from the *Oregonian/Oregon Live*; and by general operating support grants from the City of Salem's Transient Occupancy Tax funds and the Oregon Arts Commission.

Designed by Phil Kovacevich

Editorial review by Nick Allison

Proofread by Carrie Wicks

Printed and bound in Canada by Friesens Corporation

Front/back cover and fig. 16: *Coastal Range*, from the series *And Then Again: Rifts on the Forest and Time*, 2012, screenprint and acrylic on panel, 36 × 87 inches, Gift of the artist in honor of Sue Taylor, PhD, Portland Art Museum, Portland, Oregon, © Rita Robillard, 2017.96.2. Photo: Portland Art Museum.

Frontispiece: *The Gorge I* and *The Gorge II*, from the series *Waters of March—Spring*, 2019, screenprint and acrylic on panel, 48 × 24 inches each, courtesy of the artist and the Augen Gallery. Photo: Dale Peterson.

Page 4: *Deluge* (detail), from the series *Polarities: Patterns in Time: 1880/2016, 2.3 Degrees Fahrenheit*, 2016, screenprint on paper, 22 × 30 inches, collection of the Hallie Ford Museum of Art, Willamette University, Salem, Oregon, gift of the artist, 2018.014. Photo: Dan Kvitka.

Photo credits: Katie Babb, pp. 10, 31, 32, 35, 86; Bill Bachhuber, pp. 21, 65, 80; Dan Kvitka, pp. 4, 9, 27, 28, 29, 30, 36, 45, 47, 62, 73, 74–75, 77, 95; Paul Lee, 16, 17 (top), 51, 52, 56–57; Hart Monyatovsky, pp. 79, 91; Dale Peterson, pp. 6, 13, 14, 17 (bottom), 22, 23, 41, 42 (top), 48, 54, 60, 61, 67, 68; Portland Art Museum, cover, pp. 25, 69; Rita Robillard, pp. 42 (bottom); Brandon Sorg, pp. 19, 24, 59; Richard Strode, p. 71; and courtesy of the artist, pp. 12, 18, 38, 43, 44, 50, 55, 58, 72, 82, 92, 94

© 2023 by the Hallie Ford Museum of Art at Willamette University

Essays © 2023 by Bean Gilsdorf, Frances DeVuono, Patricia Grieve Watkinson, and Linda Tesner

All rights reserved. No part of this publication may be reproduced or transmitted in any form or by any means, electronic or mechanical, including photocopy, recording, or any information or retrieval system, without permission in writing from the publisher.

Library of Congress Control Number
ISBN 9781930957862

Distributed by Oregon State University Press
Corvallis, Oregon